DATE DUE

Biographies

IN AMERICAN FOREIGN POLICY

Joseph A. Fry, University of Nevada, Las Vegas
Series Editor

The Biographies in American Foreign Policy Series employs the enduring medium of biography to examine the major episodes and themes in the history of U.S. foreign relations. By viewing policy formation and implementation from the perspective of influential participants, the series seeks to humanize and make more accessible those decisions and events that sometimes appear abstract or distant. Particular attention is devoted to those aspects of the subject's background, personality, and intellect that most influenced his or her approach to U.S. foreign policy, and each individual's role is placed in a context that takes into account domestic affairs, national interests and policies, and international and strategic considerations.

The series is directed primarily at undergraduate and graduate courses in U.S. foreign relations, but it is hoped that the genre and format may also prove attractive to the interested general reader. With these objectives in mind, the length of the volumes has been kept manageable, the documentation has been restricted to direct quotes and particularly controversial assertions, and the bibliographic essays have been tailored to provide historiographical assessment without tedium.

Producing books of high scholarly merit to appeal to a wide range of readers is an ambitious undertaking, and an excellent group of authors has agreed to participate. Some have compiled extensive scholarly records while others are just beginning promising careers, but all are distinguished by their comprehensive knowledge of U.S. foreign relations, their cooperative spirit, and their enthusiasm for the project. It has been a distinct pleasure to have been given the opportunity to work with these scholars as well as with Richard Hopper and his staff at Scholarly Resources.

Volumes Published

Lawrence S. Kaplan, *Thomas Jefferson: Westward the Course of Empire* (1999). Cloth ISBN 0-8420-2629-0   Paper ISBN 0-8420-2630-4

Richard H. Immerman, *John Foster Dulles: Piety, Pragmatism, and Power in U.S. Foreign Policy* (1999). Cloth ISBN 0-8420-2600-2 Paper ISBN 0-8420-2601-0

Thomas W. Zeiler, *Dean Rusk: Defending the American Mission Abroad* (2000). Cloth ISBN 0-8420-2685-1   Paper ISBN 0-8420-2686-X

Edward P. Crapol, *James G. Blaine: Architect of Empire* (2000). Cloth ISBN 0-8420-2604-5   Paper ISBN 0-8420-2605-3

David F. Schmitz, *Henry L. Stimson: The First Wise Man* (2001). Cloth ISBN 0-8420-2631-2   Paper ISBN 0-8420-2632-0

Thomas M. Leonard, *James K. Polk: A Clear and Unquestionable Destiny* (2001). Cloth ISBN 0-8420-2646-0   Paper ISBN 0-8420-2647-9

James E. Lewis Jr., *John Quincy Adams: Policymaker for the Union* (2001). Cloth ISBN 0-8420-2622-3   Paper ISBN 0-8420-2623-1

JOHN QUINCY ADAMS

JOHN QUINCY ADAMS

Policymaker for the Union

JAMES E. LEWIS JR.

Biographies

IN AMERICAN FOREIGN POLICY

Number 7

A Scholarly Resources Inc. Imprint
Wilmington, Delaware

Scholarly Resources Inc.
104 Greenhill Avenue
Wilmington, DE 19805-1897
www.scholarly.com

Library of Congress Cataloging-in-Publication Data

Lewis, James E., 1964–
    John Quincy Adams : policymaker for the Union / James E.
      Lewis Jr.
      p. cm. — (Biographies in American foreign policy ; no. 7)
    Includes bibliographical references and index.
    ISBN 0-8420-2622-3 (cloth : alk. paper) — ISBN 0-8420-2623-1
(pbk. : alk. paper)
    1. Adams, John Quincy, 1767–1848—Contributions in diplo-
macy. 2. United States—Foreign relations—1783–1865. 3. United
States—Politics and government—1783–1865. 4. Statesmen—
United States—Biography. 5. Presidents—United States—
Biography. I. Title. II. Series.

E377.L47 2001
973.5'5'092—dc21
[B]   00-049664

For my mother and father,

Ann Fear and Jim Lewis

About the Author

James E. Lewis Jr. is the author of *The American Union and the Problem of Neighborhood: The United States and the Collapse of the Spanish Empire, 1783–1829* (1998). He received his doctorate from the University of Virginia and has taught at Hollins University, Louisiana State University, Widener University, and the University of Pennsylvania.

Contents

Acknowledgments, **xi**

Introduction, **xiii**

Chronology, **xix**

1   The Education of John Quincy Adams, 1767–1807, **1**

2   The Storms of War and Peace, 1807–1817, **21**

3   A Dangerous Neighborhood, 1817–1821, **43**

4   A Frustrating World, 1821–1825, **71**

5   A Troubled Presidency, 1825–1829, **99**

6   An Unexpected Career, 1829–1848, **119**

Conclusion, **141**

Bibliographic Essay, **147**

Index, **161**

Acknowledgments

This book would look very different if I had not previously written *The American Union and the Problem of Neighborhood*. In fairness, all of the individuals and institutions whom I thanked and acknowledged in that book deserve a mention in this one as well. In the interest of space, however, I will trust that they know who they are.

My particular thanks must go to Andy Fry for inviting me to contribute to this series, ignoring my occasional delays, and providing me with regular encouragement. If that were not enough, Andy also gave the manuscript an extremely close and valuable reading. I also received an insightful and helpful reading from another author in this series, Ed Crapol, whom I have known as a teacher and a friend since my days at the College of William and Mary nearly twenty years ago. The people at Scholarly Resources, particularly Richard Hopper and Michelle Slavin, with whom I have worked most closely, have invariably been professional and friendly.

This book would have been completed much more quickly but for my dog, Cassidy; of course, my life would have been much poorer without him. He deserves special thanks for not eating any of the notes for *this* book. In contrast, it would never have been completed but for the support—of every imaginable kind—of my wife, Charlene.

I have dedicated this book to my parents, Ann Fear and Jim Lewis. I was encouraged by them to read, ask questions, think, research, and write beginning at a very early age. This love of learning was one of the greatest gifts ever given to me. I consider myself extremely fortunate to have them still in my life and still urging me to learn more.

Introduction

That John Quincy Adams was the greatest American secretary of state has been accepted as nearly indisputable by diplomatic historians. As secretary of state under President James Monroe from 1817 to 1825, Adams confronted long-standing disputes and emerging challenges, external dangers and internal crises. The agreements that he negotiated and the policies that he developed secured peace for the present, reduced tensions for the future, furthered American territorial expansion across the continent, and promoted American commercial expansion around the globe. Some of the highlights of his eight years of service included the Convention of 1818, which fixed the border between the United States and British Canada from the Lake of the Woods to the Rocky Mountains; the Transcontinental Treaty, which gave the United States Spanish Florida and a stronger claim to the Pacific Northwest; the formal recognition of the Spanish American nations as independent states; and the Monroe Doctrine. In the view of the author of one of the leading diplomatic history textbooks, "Without doubt, John Quincy Adams remains the nation's greatest secretary of state because of his accomplishments during those years."[1]

But Adams's involvement in the formation and implementation of American foreign policy extended far beyond his eight years as secretary of state. He had already accompanied his father, John Adams, on two diplomatic missions to France before he commenced his first formal diplomatic service as the private secretary for the American minister to Russia in 1782, at just fourteen years of age. Over the next sixty-six years, he served the cause of U.S. foreign relations in a variety of posts: private secretary for his father in France; minister to the Netherlands, Prussia, Russia, and Great Britain; senator; peace commissioner at Ghent; secretary of state; president; and, finally, congressman. Even during the brief periods when he did not hold public office, he continued to try to shape policy by writing essays for newspapers and letters to federal officials.

He remained active to the end. Just days before his death in February 1848, an eighty-year-old John Quincy Adams delivered his final vote against the Mexican War in the House of Representatives.

Historians have attributed Adams's greatness as secretary of state to a number of factors. They have frequently stressed his detailed knowledge of European affairs and direct experience with diplomatic practices that derived from his long and varied service. They have also pointed to a work ethic that allowed him to be better prepared than many of his adversaries and to achieve more during his time in office. They have repeatedly highlighted his clear understanding of the conditions of the world and the interests of the nation. As a foreign policymaker, in general, and as secretary of state, in particular, moreover, Adams has been depicted as playing a critical role in defining and establishing what one historian has called "the foundations of American foreign policy." As presented by the standard accounts, Adams's greatness as secretary of state is like the greatness of a grandmaster at chess—a genius for both strategy and tactics, an understanding of the relationship between events in different areas, a vision for developments in the future, and an ability to outwit and outmaneuver his opponents. Ascribing to Adams this kind of mastery makes him into the American counterpart of the great European diplomatic statesmen of his era—Austria's Prince Metternich or Great Britain's Viscount Castlereagh.[2]

In fact, Adams was not, and could not have been, an American Metternich or Castlereagh because the United States was not, and was not intended to be, an Austria or Great Britain. Far better than later historians, Adams recognized the profound impact that the differences between the federal republic of the United States and the centralized monarchies of Europe had upon the practice and purposes of diplomacy. As Adams and many of his contempories realized, it was more difficult in the United States than in the European nations to separate foreign and domestic policies, to construct policies in a system that divided power among various levels and branches of government, and to implement these policies without infringing upon the rights of states or citizens. The federal and the republican aspects of the United States differentiated it from traditional states and determined Adams's policymaking.

Throughout his years as secretary of state and through most of his career as a diplomat and statesman, Adams's understanding of the nature and function of the federal union shaped his ideas and his policies. Like many Americans of his and his father's generations, Adams believed that North America could avoid duplicating Europe's experience of political, commercial, and military conflict among sovereign nations only if all of its independent states were joined into a single union. Upon this union depended the successful achievement of the principal goals of the American Revolution—national independence, republican government, commercial prosperity, and territorial expansion. At base, the Founders designed the Constitution and the federal government to protect and strengthen the union against all potential dangers. This logic effectively blurred distinctions between foreign and domestic problems and policies that appear fairly obvious to modern Americans. From this perspective, the greatest evil—that disunion would force the American states to treat each other as hostile nations—involved dangers that were simultaneously internal and external. The forces that might produce this evil could come from either inside or outside the United States. Unlike his European counterparts, Adams tried to shape "domestic" and "foreign" policies that would work together to counter the forces of division and cement the bonds of union.

At the same time, Adams recognized that, as the secretary of state in a republican government of limited powers and popular sovereignty, he could never exercise the kind of control over either the government or the people aspired to by a Metternich or a Castlereagh. Adams's greatness could not be the greatness of the grandmaster at chess for the very simple reason that he could not control the movement of his own pawns, knights, and bishops. He often lamented and occasionally sought to redress this lack of control. But, during his years as secretary of state, he found the people and the states, Congress and the Supreme Court, other cabinet members and the president, officers of the armed forces and subordinate officials of his own department undermining and thwarting his efforts to apply pressure and offer incentives as parts of the diplomatic process. In shaping foreign policy for a nontraditional American nation in a world of traditional European nations, Adams, like most of his predecessors in the State Department, sought ways to work within the conventions of European diplomacy without abandoning the distinctiveness of American republicanism.

As a commissioner to negotiate an end to the War of 1812 at Ghent, as minister to Great Britain following the war, and as secretary of state, Adams exhibited greatness. But it was not the greatness that the standard accounts attribute to him. It was more nearly the greatness of the poker—or, more aptly, whist—expert than the chess grandmaster. Adams succeeded by making the most of the cards that were dealt him, risking little on the bad hands, and understanding that he could win even with a weak hand if he played it correctly. Adams's greatness came not from controlling all of the inducements and punishments—the carrots and sticks—of diplomacy but from capitalizing on events that he could not control. And it derived from his ability to find diplomatic advantages in the very weaknesses that resulted from the nontraditional nature of the American state. By insisting that the federal government could not control the actions of citizens and states, Adams could deflect European complaints when the unchecked energies of the American people led them to new lands and new markets. The Treaty of Ghent, the Convention of 1818, and the Transcontinental Treaty—as well as other policies—made clear the wisdom of this approach.

In a larger sense, however, Adams ultimately failed as a policymaker, in general, and secretary of state, in particular—something that he repeatedly acknowledged in the two decades after his presidency. Despite his occasionally spectacular achievements when confronted with specific threats and opportunities, he failed in his underlying effort to protect and strengthen the union. Adams consistently acted upon his belief that a single union was essential for American happiness, that federal action was essential for lasting union, and that foreign and domestic issues were essentially indivisible. First as secretary of state and then as president, he tried to instill this belief in policymakers, politicians, and the public as unquestioned, and unquestionable, assumptions. By the end of his presidency, however, most Americans considered Adams's thinking hopelessly, perhaps even dangerously, outmoded. They believed that the union was safe, that federal efforts to strengthen it involved unnecessary sacrifices of their interests and unsafe threats to their liberties, and that a clear division separated foreign and domestic policies and problems. Worse yet, some of Adams's policies—especially territorial expansion—took on a life that was separate from, and even contrary to, their original logic. When he died in early 1848, expansion into Texas, New Mexico, and California had pushed the union into its deepest crisis yet and created the issues that would lead to the secession and civil war that Adams had considered increasingly likely during the preceding two decades.

Over the course of his long career as a policymaker, Adams experienced both success and failure, triumph and disappointment. In order to assess his policymaking accurately, it is necessary to understand, as Adams understood, that the purposes and the processes of diplomacy in the early years of the United States had to reflect its federal and republican system.

Notes

1. Walter LaFeber, *The American Age: United States Foreign Policy at Home and Abroad since 1750* (New York, 1989), 72. Other historians who share this view include Samuel Flagg Bemis, *John Quincy Adams and the Foundations of American Foreign Policy* (New York, 1949), 571; Norman A. Graebner, "John Quincy Adams and the Federalist Tradition," in *Foundations of American Foreign Policy: A Realist Appraisal from Franklin to McKinley* (Wilmington, Del., 1985), 145–79; William Earl Weeks, *John Quincy Adams and American Global Empire* (Lexington, Ky., 1992), 1; and H. William Brands, *The United States in the World: A History of American Foreign Policy* (Boston, 1994), 102–3.

2. Bemis, *Adams and the Foundations*, 567. For comparisons with Castlereagh, see Bradford Perkins, *Castlereagh and Adams: England and the United States, 1812–1823* (Berkeley, Calif., 1964); and Brands, *United States in the World*, 101–2.

Chronology

1767

July 11	Born, Braintree (now Quincy), Massachusetts, to John and Abigail Adams

1778

February	Sailed for France with his father

1779

August	Returned to Boston with his father
November	Sailed with his father for Spain and the Netherlands; began keeping a diary

1781

July	Left for St. Petersburg as secretary for Francis Dana, minister to Russia

1783

April	Returned to the Netherlands and, later, France to serve as his father's secretary

1785

July	Returned to Massachusetts to study for entrance into Harvard College

1787

July 16	Graduated from Harvard second in his class; delivered one of the commencement addresses
September	Moved to Newburyport, Massachusetts, to study law

1790

July	Moved to Boston and opened his own law office

1793

April	Began publishing "Marcellus" essays
November	Began publishing "Columbus" essays

1794

May 30	Appointed minister to the Netherlands by President George Washington
September	Sailed for the Netherlands, stopping en route in London, where he observed the final stages of Jay's Treaty negotiations

1795

November	Returned to London for the final ratification of Jay's Treaty; became engaged to Louisa Catherine Johnson, the daughter of the U.S. consul

1796

May 28	Appointed minister to Portugal by President Washington, later changed to Prussia by his father

1797

July 26	Married Louisa Catherine Johnson in London
November	Arrived in Prussia

1799

July 11	Signed Prussian-American commercial treaty

1801

February 3	Recalled from Prussia by his father a month before Thomas Jefferson's inauguration
April 13	First son, George Washington Adams, born in Berlin
September	Returned to Boston to resume legal practice

1802

April 5	Elected to Massachusetts state senate
November 3	Lost election as Federalist candidate to represent the Boston District in the House of Representatives by fifty-nine votes

1803

February 8	Elected to U.S. Senate by Federalists in Massachusetts legislature
July 4	Second son, John Adams II, born
October	Supported Louisiana Purchase, the only Federalist senator to do so

1806

February	Helped write Senate resolutions criticizing British maritime policies; was the only Federalist senator to vote for the Non-Importation Act

1807

July 10	Attended Republican town meeting in Boston to protest the British attack on the USS *Chesapeake*
August 18	Third son, Charles Francis Adams, born
December 18	Voted for the Embargo

1808

January	Attended Republican presidential caucus
May	Federalists in Massachusetts legislature elected Adams's successor as senator six months early
June 8	Resigned his Senate seat upon learning of the state legislature's action

1809

March 6	Appointed minister to Russia by President James Madison
August	Sailed for Russia with Louisa Catherine and Charles Francis, leaving the two older sons with their grandparents in Quincy

1811

April	Nominated and confirmed as associate justice of the Supreme Court; declined appointment
August 12	Only daughter, Louisa Adams, born in St. Petersburg

1812

September 15	Daughter died

1814

January	Appointed to peace commission to negotiate an end to the War of 1812
August	Peace talks began at Ghent, Belgium
December 24	Treaty of Ghent signed

1815

May 7	Appointed minister to Great Britain

July 3   Signed, with Henry Clay and Albert Gallatin, the commercial Convention of 1815 with Great Britain

1817

March 6   Appointed secretary of state by President James Monroe

August   Returned to the United States

September 22 Sworn in as secretary of state

1818

October 20   Convention of 1818 with Great Britain signed by Richard Rush and Albert Gallatin

October 28   Mother died

1819

February 22   Transcontinental Treaty with Spain completed

1821

February 22   Transcontinental Treaty finally ratified

July 4   Delivered Fourth of July oration in Congress

1822

February   Nominated for the presidency by Massachusetts legislature

March   President Monroe effectively recognized five Spanish American nations in a message to Congress

June 24   Commercial agreement signed with France

August 24   British ships from West Indies allowed to enter U.S. ports by presidential proclamation

1823

December 2   Monroe Doctrine announced to Congress in annual message

1824

May   Submitted slave trade convention with Great Britain to Senate, where it was heavily amended

November   Received 84 electoral and 105,321 popular votes in presidential election, but no one received a majority of the electoral votes

1825

January 11	Exchanged ratifications of Northwest Coast convention with Russian minister
February 9	Elected president on first ballot by House of Representatives
March 4	Inaugurated as sixth president
December 5	Sent first annual message to Congress
December 25	Commercial treaty signed with Central American federation
December 26	Nominated Richard C. Anderson and John Sergeant as ministers to Panama Congress

1826

March 14	Senate finally confirmed appointments of Anderson and Sergeant
July 4	Father died
Fall	Midterm congressional elections strengthened antiadministration forces

1827

August 6	Anglo-American convention extended joint occupation of Oregon country indefinitely

1828

May 19	Signed into law "Tariff of Abominations"
July 4	Broke ground for Chesapeake and Ohio Canal
October	Entered into a controversy with New England Federalists over disunionist sentiment after the Louisiana Purchase
November	Received 83 electoral and 508,065 popular votes in presidential election; defeated by Andrew Jackson

1829

March 3	Moved out of President's Mansion one day before Jackson's inauguration
April 30	Oldest son, George Washington, died, probably suicide
June	Returned to Quincy to begin his retirement

1830

September	Asked if he would serve in Congress
November 1	Elected to House of Representatives from the Plymouth District of Massachusetts;

	reelected every two years for the rest of his life

1831

July 4	Delivered Fourth of July oration in Quincy denouncing nullification
December 5	Took seat in Congress

1832

May	Helped arrange compromise tariff

1833

November 11	Defeated as Anti-Masonic candidate for governor of Massachusetts

1834

October 23	Second son, John, died

1835

March	Defended Jackson's stand against France

1836

May	Led congressional attack against the annexation of Texas

1837

February	Led protest against "gag rule"

1841

February 24	Appeared before Supreme Court to argue *Amistad* case
December	Appointed chairman of House Foreign Affairs Committee

1842

January 25– February 5	Defended himself against Democratic attempt to censure and expel him

1844

October	Delivered fiery address to Young Men's Whig Club of Boston
December 7	Finally succeeded in repealing "gag rule"

1845

February	Voted against joint resolution to annex Texas

1846

January	Spoke out in Congress in favor of 54°40' border for Oregon
May 11	Voted against Mexican War

1848

February 21	Suffered a stroke on the floor of the House
February 23	Died at the Capitol
March 11	Buried at Quincy

1

The Education of
John Quincy Adams

1767–1807

John Quincy Adams grew up with the country. He was
born a British subject in the colony of Massachusetts,
but turned ten an American citizen of the state of Massachusetts. At the time of his twentieth birthday in July 1787,
delegates from twelve of the thirteen independent American states were meeting in Philadelphia to draft a new
Constitution to replace the original Articles of Confederation. He turned thirty en route to Prussia to represent
the reorganized young nation headed by his father, the
recently elected president. By his fortieth birthday in July
1807, the United States was locked in a battle of wills over
the law of nations and the rights of neutrals with the two
most powerful countries of Europe.

It was during these four decades that the United States
took shape as an independent, republican, and federal
nation and that Adams became aware of the many implications of its distinct form of government for policymaking. A half or even a full generation younger than the true
Founders, he lagged a little behind them in gaining this
awareness. What James Madison, Alexander Hamilton,
Thomas Jefferson, George Washington, and his father,
John Adams, came to understand about federal union and
republican government during the 1770s and 1780s, John
Quincy Adams grew to comprehend only during the 1790s
and the first years of the 1800s. That he had completely
accepted and adopted the thinking of the Founders was
clear, however, at least as early as his response to the Louisiana Purchase of 1803.

~

John Quincy Adams was raised for greatness. The first child of John and Abigail Adams, his birth in July 1767 came just as his father entered into prominence as a lawyer, a writer, and a patriot in the growing crisis between Great Britain and its North American colonies. With the first two decades of his life coinciding with the imperial crisis, the Revolutionary War, and the subsequent "crisis of the 1780s," John Quincy could hardly have avoided exposure to politics. But his parents insisted that he was immersed in, trained for, and committed to a life in politics. Before his eighth birthday, he and Abigail climbed to the top of a nearby hill to watch the Battle of Bunker Hill in neighboring Boston. With John in, first, Boston and, later, Philadelphia championing independence, Abigail impressed upon her young son a duty to follow the example of his father by serving his country. John Quincy's schooling in Braintree with Abigail, in Paris, Amsterdam, St. Petersburg, and The Hague with John and on his own, and at Harvard after his return from Europe in 1785 ensured that he was as well prepared for public service and political life as any twenty-year-old in the country when he graduated from college. He could have had little doubt that, at least in the eyes of his parents, his destiny was as "a Guardian of the Laws Liberty and Religion of [his] Country."[1]

Adams's upbringing and schooling in the first two decades of his life combined three elements that were not wholly compatible in the late eighteenth century and may seem even less compatible now. His parents, particularly his mother, inculcated in him the views and beliefs—religious, social, cultural, and political—of a Massachusetts Puritan. At the same time, they raised him as a student of the Enlightenment and a man of reason. Finally, they insisted that he acquire a measure of refinement and gentility. Faith and skepticism, conservativism and progressivism, elegance and simplicity, parochialism and cosmopolitanism, independence and duty all came together, at times uneasily, in the upbringing of John Quincy Adams. In the proper balance, John and Abigail believed, these values and traits would make their son the quintessential republican gentleman.

Writing as a fifth-generation Massachusetts Puritan, John instructed Abigail, in her raising of their children during his absence, to "let them revere nothing but Religion, Morality and Liberty." Massachusetts Puritans had long thought that religion, morality, and liberty were intricately interwoven. Religion, as Abigail taught

John Quincy, was "the only sure and permanant foundation of virtue"; as every good republican knew, "virtue," which included political and moral components at the time, was essential to liberty. A belief in God, "a just sense of his attributes as a Being infinately wise, just, and good," and a commitment to daily reading in the Bible formed the cornerstone of John Quincy's Puritan upbringing. His Puritan heritage also included a commitment to improving society that was supposed to guide the actions of both individuals and governments. As colony and state, Massachusetts acted on this Puritan commitment to societal improvement for more than two centuries after its founding in the 1630s. No less than his Protestant religious beliefs, this expectation that government and people would work together as a "commonwealth" to promote economic, intellectual, moral, and social progress was a key component of John Quincy's Puritan upbringing.[2]

Just as John and Abigail turned to Massachusetts Puritanism to shape their son's faith, character, and values, they looked to the Enlightenment to shape his mind. Before John Quincy's tenth birthday, his father tried to impress upon him the importance of "a Taste for Literature, includ[ing] the Love of Science and the fine Arts." Learning, John insisted, would be "of the utmost Importance to you in Business, as well as the most ingenious and elegant Entertainment, of your Life." Beginning at an early age and continuing through his graduation from Harvard, John Quincy's schooling encompassed Latin, Greek, French, and Dutch, ancient and modern history, literature, mathematics, and science. His years in Europe between 1778 and 1785 included stays at such centers of the Enlightenment as Paris, Amsterdam, and The Hague. In Europe, he filled even his free time with the pursuits proper to a man of the Enlightenment. He attended plays and concerts, viewed paintings and sculptures, and—in a classic display of the Enlightenment's fascination with scientific progress—observed a hot air balloon ascension. At Harvard, he joined the A. B. Club, whose members met regularly to present and discuss compositions in verse and prose. During these two decades, he adopted the Enlightenment's skepticism of received truths, whether political, religious, or scientific, and its confidence in future progress in politics and science resulting from an improved knowledge of natural and human laws and an increased willingness to experiment with new ideas.[3]

With some ambivalence, John and Abigail also urged their son to acquire the manners and skills appropriate to a refined gentleman. The line between the "refined few" and the "vulgar many"

formed one of the clearest divisions between those who were expected to lead and those who were expected to follow in late colonial and early national America. It was essential, given his parents'
expectations, that John Quincy be on the right side of that line.
Refinement required learning to dance, dine, speak, write, walk,
stand, and sit according to prescribed rules; it also meant being
able to discuss, in person or by letter, the topics appropriate to po-
lite society; and it involved attending balls, concerts, teas, dinners,
and plays with other gentlemen and ladies. John repeatedly pushed
his son to improve both the handwriting and the style of his letters. He also encouraged him to practice dancing, horseback riding,
and skating as ways to acquire "an Elegance of Motion, which is
charming to the sight." Yet there was always a danger. Gentility
had its origins and reached its zenith in the courts of Europe's
monarchies. Father and son both worried that, carried to an excess,
the commitment to refinement threatened the simplicity and virtue essential to republican government. "Whenever Vanity, and
Gaiety, a Love of Pomp and Dress, Furniture, Equipage, Buildings,
great Company, expensive Diversions, and elegant Entertainments
get the better of the Principles and Judgments of Men or Women,"
John remarked to Abigail early in the revolutionary struggle, "there
is no knowing where they will stop, nor into what Evils, natural,
moral, or political, they will lead us."[4]

Taken together, his schooling at home with his mother, his trav-
els in Europe alone and with his father, and his education at Harvard
formed John Quincy Adams into the educated, Christian, republican gentleman that his parents had hoped he would become. John
and Abigail realized that they had taken risks. Europe and college,
they believed, would try their son's faith, morals, and republicanism. Abigail viewed the university as a place where "infidelity
abounds, both in example and precepts." Young men succumbed
to doubting their religious beliefs "and from doubting to disbe-
lief." Europe similarly lured impressionable young men with its
immoral dissipation and aristocratic principles. After John Quincy
had spent five years there, Abigail expressed her hope that he had
"not imbibe[d] any sentiments or principals which will not be
agreable to the Laws the Goverment and Religion of our own Country." Her son shared some of these concerns. In his first year at
Harvard, he admitted his "fear[s] that by having received so large
a share of my education in Europe, my attachment to a republican
government would not be sufficient for pleasing my countrymen."
What he discovered instead, however, was "that [he was] the best

republican here." When he graduated in July 1787, it seemed clear that his parents' fears had been groundless. At the commencement ceremony, he delivered an oration, "Upon the importance and necessity of public faith, to the well-being of a Community," that emphasized the need for virtue, morality, and simplicity in a republican government.[5]

John Quincy Adams may have been raised to be a republican gentleman, but he had not fully become one when he graduated from Harvard. A republican gentleman had to be independent. Economic independence—supporting one's self and one's family by one's own effort—was deemed essential for political independence—making one's own decisions about voting and policies. The twenty-year-old Adams lacked this independence. He expected to need three years of studying law in the office of an established lawyer and another three or four years of developing his practice before he would be able to provide for himself financially. The limits to Adams's independence extended far beyond his finances. He had entered into the law because his father saw that as the next step in his training as a statesman. John Quincy had little desire to become a lawyer and not much more to become a statesman. While on diplomatic business in Paris in 1780, his father had written, somewhat metaphorically: "I must study Politicks and War that my sons may have liberty to study Mathematicks and Philosophy. My sons ought to study Mathematicks and Philosophy . . . , in order to give their Children a right to study Painting, Poetry, Musick, Architecture, Statuary, Tapestry and Porcelaine." In the late 1780s and early 1790s, John Quincy often wanted, in a sense, to skip one generation by becoming a poet or author. Instead, he succumbed to the tremendous pressure from his parents to do as his father had done by studying "Politicks and War."[6]

~

John Quincy Adams learned a lot during his years in Europe and at Harvard before July 1787, although he did not learn what many American statesmen were learning about the shortcomings of the government established by the Articles of Confederation. As he graduated from Harvard, delegates from twelve American states were meeting in Philadelphia as a constitutional convention in an effort "to form a more perfect union." Adams initially opposed the fruits of their labors—the federal Constitution. Over the course of the late 1780s and early 1790s, however, political divisions at home and military conflict in Europe convinced him of the wisdom of the Founders, even as they brought him to accept his destiny as a diplomat and a statesman. In time, his discussions of the functions of the federal union and the limits of its republican government differed little from those of the Constitution's early advocates. Like Washington and his father, he prescribed harmony at home and neutrality toward Europe as essential for the union. Like them, he became a Federalist. But his fierce independence—and his family loyalties—always limited his commitment to the Federalists and, especially, to their leading thinker, Alexander Hamilton.

In the summer of 1787, Adams, along with the delegates at the constitutional convention, thought about the problems that faced the states and the nation. His solution, as developed in his commencement address, required a greater display of "those severe republican virtues" of patriotism and self-sacrifice. As Adams reiterated the plea for greater virtue, the framers of the Constitution devised a system that could accommodate less virtue. They crafted checks and balances among the three branches of the federal government, restricted the powers of the more democratic states, and distanced elected officials from the voters. Where Adams's oration largely ignored the problems between the states and between the United States and other powers, the new Constitution attempted to strengthen the bonds of union and the powers of the central government. Adams initially opposed the Constitution because it seemed to abandon the republican ideals of the Revolution and acknowledge "that a free government is inconsistent with human nature." Its ratification, he concluded, would "be a grand point gained in favour of the aristocratic party" since "it [was] calculated to increase the influence, power and wealth of those who [had] any already." When Massachusetts's ratifying convention approved the Constitution, Adams noted that he was "now converted, though not convinced"; he would back the new government as the will of the majority, but still did not approve of it himself.[7]

Adams grew convinced as a result of developments at home and abroad over the next few years. In the first years under the new Constitution, its original advocates divided over a number of commercial, financial, and economic issues into Federalists, who supported Secretary of the Treasury Hamilton, and Republicans, who backed Secretary of State Jefferson and Congressman Madison. This division among policymakers spread to the public in early 1793 when war erupted between republican France and monarchical Great Britain. In the cities and in the South and West, most of the people supported France and the Republicans; in the Northeast, most of the people preferred Great Britain and the Federalists. Like many of his contemporaries, Adams worried that either France or Great Britain could exploit the domestic factionalism to destroy the young republic. "It was the interference of other nations in their domestic divisions," Adams explained in a series of essays that he published under the pseudonym "Columbus" in late 1793, that had been fatal to ancient and modern republics. The situation of the United States seemed especially alarming because the political divisions—whether resulting from domestic or foreign concerns—so closely followed geographic lines. The collapse of the union under the strain of these divisions and conflicts appeared increasingly likely to Adams over the course of the 1790s, just as it had to the Founders over the course of the 1780s. In this new crisis, he came to understand many of the fears that had led them to draft the Constitution.[8]

At the same time, Adams struggled through a personal crisis. He had completed his legal training and opened his own law office in Boston in the summer of 1790. While he did not enjoy being a lawyer, his practice did allow him to support himself by early 1794, starting him toward the independence needed by a republican gentleman. Even though he felt compelled to make known his views on the political issues of his day, he limited his participation to pseudonymous columns in the newspapers. A life in politics—the life for which he had been prepared—sounded increasingly unappealing. Becoming "a public man," he worried, "would throw me completely in the power of the people, and all my future life would be a life of dependence." His hesitancy and uncertainty led to renewed pressure from his father, the vice president. "If you do not rise to the head not only of your Profession but of your Country," John Adams told his son in April 1794, "it will be owing to your own *Laziness Slovenliness* and *Obstinacy*." In what seems to have finally been a concerted effort to break free of his parents' expectations, John Quincy replied that he had "every day less ambition than the former, to pursue a political career." He was, he insisted, "contented with my state as it is." The same day that he wrote to his father foreswearing a political life, however, his father wrote to him announcing that President Washington had nominated him as minister to the Netherlands. His father's "satisfaction at the appointment," John Quincy noted in his diary, "is much greater than mine[;] I rather wish it had not been made at all."[9]

While minister to, first, the Netherlands and, then, Prussia between 1794 and 1801, Adams evinced his changed understanding of the Constitution. He had abandoned his early opposition to the Constitution as a counterrevolutionary document and adopted the Founders' argument that a more perfect union was essential for achieving the fundamental goals of the Revolution. National independence, republican government, commercial prosperity, and territorial expansion—Madison, Hamilton, and other supporters of the Constitution had insisted—would prove unattainable unless a single political union joined all of the American states, and a stronger central government commanded respect from other powers. The domestic divisions and external pressures of the early 1790s only intensified during Adams's years abroad. The party battles grew more fierce as Federalists and Republicans refused to associate, socialize, or even do business with each other. At the same time, France and Great Britain increasingly tried "to draw [the United States] into the vortex" of war by manipulating both a public divided over European developments and a commercial sector interested in new markets. Only by promoting union, Adams repeatedly warned, could Americans secure their independence and their republicanism.[10]

Like the Founders, Adams centered his hopes for national independence on the preservation of the union and considered "its dissolution . . . the most dreadful of our dangers." He looked to a union of the states both to concentrate the resources and manpower needed to defend against a foreign invasion and to check the opportunities for foreign interference. The union, as Adams explained to his brother in 1801, eliminated the need for a large standing army in a country where the rapid growth of wealth and population brought new strength with each passing year. If the union divided, however, the American people would find their "exposure to foreign assault" increased "in proportion to the number of states into which [they] split, and aggravated in proportion to the weakness of every single part." Individual states or partial confederacies, Adams argued, would provide tempting targets for foreign invasion once disunion increased "the prospect of success." At the same time, dissolving the union would invite European interference. Each state would turn to Europe in search of assistance against its American neighbors. Adams predicted that the different states would eventually find themselves "swayed by rival European powers, whose policy [would] agree perfectly in the system of keeping us at variance with one another." With disunion, the states would be recolonized in effect if not in form, partitioned among the major powers, and immersed in Europe's wars. If they allowed the union to break, Americans would sink to a condition worse than that before the Revolution.[11]

Yet the increased danger of foreign interference was "not the worst" consequence of a dissolution of the union according to Adams. "From the moment of disunion," he recognized, each of the independent states or partial confederacies would "become with regard to the others a foreign power." These independent states, of course, would quarrel over boundaries, commerce, and other issues, just as the multiple independent states of Europe had for centuries. The end of the republican experiment in America would follow necessarily, Adams, like the Founders, argued. The threat of war between the states would force each to maintain the armed forces, fortresses, and walled cities required for its self-preservation. But, "standing armies, intolerable taxes, forced levies, contributions, conscriptions, and requisitions" seemed incompatible with republican government to most Americans. In order to support these measures, "principles and measures of continual compulsion upon the people" would prove necessary just as they had throughout Europe. In time, the dictates of self-preservation would force Americans to abandon their relatively weak republics for more energetic monarchies or aristocracies. North America would replicate Europe, whose combination of "a number of wholly independent states" and a balance-of-power state system had condemned it to tyrannical governments and frequent wars. The thinking of the Founders and the experience of Europe at war convinced Adams that the same fate awaited North America at the end of "the unavoidable and fatal chain of which disunion [was] but the first link."[12]

For Adams, as for the leading policymakers of the Federalist and Republican parties, disunion posed the greatest threat to the young nation. Foreign powers "may distress us," he reminded his father in early 1794, "but we can be ruined only by ourselves." The danger of disunion, Adams realized, was rooted in the great diversity of interests in the union and the unfortunate grouping of these interests along sectional lines. Without this uneven distribution, the competition between farmers, merchants, and manufacturers, or between creditors and debtors, or between pro-French and pro-British, or between Federalists and Republicans might have worked, as Madison had predicted in *The Federalist*, to secure republican government against the dangers of minority or majority factions.

Instead, the clash of interests threatened to tear the still-fragile union apart as new developments, whether at home or abroad, intensified the conflict between them. Even before he received his posting to the Netherlands in 1794, Adams had concluded that "to conciliate and unite" was "the interest and duty of every American," especially of every policymaker.[13]

In Adams's thinking, reducing party conflict at home and maintaining strict neutrality in Europe's wars were the essential policies for conciliating different interests and uniting diverse sections. He had called for such measures in his "Marcellus" and "Columbus" essays of 1793. He renewed this advice in his reports to the State Department and letters to his father from The Hague in 1795. His views received their clearest expression at this time not in his own writings, however, but in Washington's famous Farewell Address of 1796. Washington had read Adams's essays and reports, had been impressed by them, and had even borrowed some of Adams's phrases for his address. After reading a copy of the address, Adams made clear to the outgoing president his belief that Washington's advice of unity at home and neutrality abroad should "serve as the foundation upon which the whole system of [the United States's] future policy [should] rise." He hoped that the popular hero's "warning voice" would serve to "control the fury of domestic factions and check the encroachments of foreign influence." Throughout the rest of his stay in Europe, he often referred to Washington's address to bolster his own advice and concerns. Still, he feared that, despite the first president's efforts, "the system of neutrality in all the wars of Europe in which [the United States] have no concern" still faced opposition at home. And he recognized, especially in the midst of the explosive election of 1800, that "the spirit of faction reign[ed] with unabated virulence." Most alarmingly, the people still had not fully accepted "the indispensable necessity of the national union for the welfare of all."[14]

Over the course of the 1790s, Adams also gradually realized that republicanism, like federalism, affected the formation and implementation of policy in the United States in ways that would always distinguish it, to some degree, from traditional European nations. Initially, he had thought otherwise. His earliest discussions of American neutrality in the "Marcellus" essays of 1793 had insisted that the rights and obligations of neutrals were defined by "immutable laws of justice and equity, which [were] equally obligatory to sovereigns and to subjects, to republics and to kings." Whether republican or monarchical, in other words, governments that claimed neutrality in a war could be held to the same "line of conduct" by the belligerent parties. In order for the United States to enjoy its rights as a neutral, Adams had further argued, it must meet its duties as a neutral. At a time when Americans were taking French privateering licenses in order to prey upon British ships, he insisted that the federal government had to "disavow in the most decisive manner, all acts of iniquity committed by our own citizens" and "compel" citizens whose actions violated neutrality "to make compensation." In the early 1790s, Adams viewed the United States as a nation that both should and could act like other nations in its relations with the rest of the world and its dealings with its own citizens.[15]

For the rest of the decade, Adams continued to believe that the United States *should* act as other nations did, but he quickly came to doubt that it *could* do so. Americans had "committed many great errors," he noted in 1798, "in confounding the principles of internal government with those of external relations." In his thinking, limiting the powers of the government internally did not automatically mean limiting its powers internationally. Most Americans, however, thought otherwise. Republicanism led them to "dread the force of the executive power at home." As a result, they left the federal government "without any power to withstand force from abroad." Early in the Quasi-War with France, Adams cautioned that such political "prejudices" threatened to "tear from us every weapon of defence." Even in the midst of a war crisis, the federal government met fierce opposition when it tried to expand the army and establish a navy. It was equally apparent that the government could not "exact obedience" from its citizens, particularly when it meant restraining their "boundless avidity" to pursue economic gain. Even the regular operations of diplomacy were affected by republicanism, Adams discovered while on his European missions. Private, coded letters from American ministers abroad to the secretary of state found their way to the public since the government had "no more retention than a sieve." After repeated complaints to the State Department, Adams finally conceded in the summer of 1798 "that secrecy is not understood to be a property of good government with us."[16]

Much had happened to Adams, personally and politically, by the time that he returned from Europe in the fall of 1801. His private life had been transformed when he met Louisa Catherine Johnson, the daughter of the American consul in London. They married in the summer of 1797 and, though their relationship was strained at times, remained together until his death more than fifty years later. Their first child, George Washington Adams, was born in the spring of 1801. Furthermore, by this time, John Quincy appears to have already developed in full his notoriously difficult personality. Throughout his life, he often exasperated his family, friends, and political allies. He frequently worked his way to positions on issues, personal and political, that they considered convoluted and nonsensical. Committed to appearing independent and nonpartisan, his votes and arguments occasionally seemed to his contemporaries to reflect little more than a great abhorrence of doing what was expected of him. Insisting, to himself as much as anyone else, upon the purity of his own acts, Adams could easily dismiss opposing positions as morally corrupt, politically motivated, or otherwise self-serving. As he entered upon a series of new public offices and duties after 1801, these character traits became increasingly apparent.

Between 1794 and 1801, Adams's public service to his country took him to the Netherlands and Prussia. His first ministerial assignment included few interesting or important duties, beyond the relatively mundane task of overseeing the repayment of loans that dated to the Revolutionary War. A brief side trip temporarily made him the highest-ranking American diplomat in London, though his unskillful diplomacy there did him little credit. His Prussian mission was more successful. Adams's responsibilities included revising and renewing a decade-old commercial treaty. Secretary of State Timothy Pickering charged him with bringing the treaty into line with the idea of neutral rights agreed to in Jay's Treaty. As a result, Adams had to abandon what he would later consider almost unnegotiable positions on the definition of contraband and blockades and the idea that "free ships make free goods." Two other provisions that were lost from the original treaty—a prohibition on privateering and the immunity of private property at sea in cases of war between the United States and Prussia—would reappear among Adams's policy proposals during his second term as secretary of state.

In early 1801, John Quincy Adams was recalled from Prussia by his father, the outgoing president. He had done all that had been asked of him. But his father apparently wished to save him from the embarrassment of being removed by the new, Republican president, Jefferson. Perhaps the most important thing to happen to John Quincy Adams between 1787 and 1801 was learning about the purposes and processes of American policymaking. During these years, he had come to understand and accept that "Union [was] the principle paramount to all others in the policy of every American." And he had realized "how essentially weak our government" was, and was likely to remain, as a result of its republican principles.[17]

~

All that Adams had learned and become in the preceding thirty-six years combined in his response to the Louisiana Purchase. He pursued a course that was independent of party considerations, as befit the republican gentleman that his parents had raised him to be. In fact, Adams ultimately came into collision with both parties over this issue—departing from his own party, the Federalists, by backing the purchase itself and clashing with the administration party, the Republicans, by calling for a constitutional amendment. The two facets of this response, moreover, demonstrated clearly the understanding of the federal union and its republican government that Adams had developed during the 1790s. Like most Republicans and a few Federalists, he recognized the tremendous value of the acquisition of Louisiana for the stability of the union. Like a few Republicans and some Federalists, he saw a great difficulty in accommodating the terms of the purchase to the ideals of the republic. Adams's response to the Louisiana Purchase made clear his determination to be a "man of [his] whole country," even though it seemed that the easiest road to success as "a politician in this country" demanded, instead, that he be a "man of a party."[18]

Adams found himself with an uncertain future when he and his family returned from Europe in the fall of 1801. His diplomatic assignments of the previous seven years had all come from Federalist presidents, but the Federalist candidate had lost in the recent election. The election left him bitter toward the new president and the Republicans and disillusioned about "our Constitution and Union." But he was far less embittered and disillusioned than many Federalists. He did not believe, as some Federalists did, "that it would have been better to have had [no election]." And he reasoned, as few Federalists could in 1801, that, as long as Jefferson's "object [was] to preserve" the union, "the issue of the election [would] not prove materially hurtful." He returned to practicing law and writing pseudonymous essays, often political and often for a Federalist journal, the *Port Folio*. In April 1802, he was elected to the Massachusetts state senate; the following February, he was elected by the state legislature to the United States Senate. Though the Federalists retained their control over Massachusetts, Adams quickly realized that they had permanently lost influence over the nation. He saw that "there never was a system of measures more completely and irrevocably abandoned and rejected by the popular voice" than that of the Federalists. "To attempt its restoration," he suggested, "would be as absurd as to undertake the resurrection of a carcase seven years in its grave." When he arrived in the new capital city of Washington, D.C., to assume his duties as a senator, Adams would represent a minority party and a declining state; the first issue that required his attention in the fall of 1803 was the Louisiana Purchase.[19]

Adams had been thinking about the vast province of Louisiana for years before the fall of 1803, but his early views deviated somewhat from his eventual support for the purchase. In February 1797 while stationed in the Netherlands, he had reported to his father on French interest in reacquiring Louisiana from Spain. At the time, he had speculated about possible connections between the French in Louisiana and Americans in the trans-Appalachian West leading to unneutral attacks on British or Spanish colonies in the Western Hemisphere. Four years later, concerns about the union, rather than about neutrality, shaped his initial response to rumors of a treaty transfering Louisiana and perhaps East and West Florida from Spain to France. "I feel very indifferent whether Louisiana and the Floridas belong to France or Spain," he confessed at a time when many policymakers viewed this matter with horror. Instead of worrying that a French possession of Louisiana "would give them *influence* over us," he expected that "it would raise clashing interests to counteract too great an influence." The French "system of liberating slaves and of shackling trade" would alienate, not attract, "southern planters." Furthermore, "the natural antipathies of borderers," made even more powerful by France's control of "the mouth of the Mississippi," would "kindl[e] animosities" that would limit its influence. "Let them take Louisiana," Adams concluded, trusting that it would propel the South and West into a closer union with anti-French New England.[20]

Nonetheless, Adams viewed the eventual Louisiana Purchase as "of the highest advantage" to the United States, a position that separated him from every other Federalist in the Senate and most of them in New England. A series of delays on the road from Boston prevented him from reaching Washington for the start of the special session of Congress that Jefferson called for October 1803.

When he finally arrived three days late, he found that the Senate had already voted in favor of the treaty, 24 to 7. Adams had missed his opportunity to cast the only Federalist vote for the treaty. But it was soon widely known that he approved of the purchase. To the other Federalist senators (who represented three New England states and Delaware), the Louisiana Purchase was an immense waste of government funds and a grave threat to the sectional balance carefully crafted by the constitutional convention. Adams acknowledged that, once admitted to the union as states, "the whole weight and power of the purchased territories [would] be thrown into the scale of southern and western influence" in a way "never contemplated" by the Founders. He wondered whether the purchase would finally "prove a blessing or a curse to this Union." But he thought that the vast majority of the people, even in New England, approved of the treaty and believed that it was the duty of the Federalist minority, "as good citizens," to acquiesce. Unbeknownst to Adams, some of his Federalist colleagues' opposition to the purchase was so vehement that they spent the winter discussing a secessionist scheme to take New England and New York out of the union.[21]

It was not simply that Adams supported a measure that most Federalists opposed; he even supported it for the same reasons as most Republicans. His support reflected the same fears about the fragile bonds between East and West that had motivated most Republicans, including President Jefferson and Secretary of State Madison. Adams found especially persuasive a speech by Kentucky Senator John Breckinridge that warned of a "danger to the Union" if Congress "abandon[ed] near a million of [its] Western citizens to ruin and despair" by rejecting the treaty and accepting French control of the Mississippi River. Adams insisted that even a westerner such as Breckinridge could not believe more strongly than himself in "the immense importance to this Union of the possession of the ceded country." But Adams identified a problem that Breckinridge dismissed. The acquisition of Louisiana might weaken, as well as strengthen, the union. It would certainly strengthen the union between the trans-Appalachian West and the Atlantic states by securing the use of the Mississippi. But it might, at the same time, "endanger the Union itself, by the expansion of its bulk, and the enfeebling extension of its line of defence against foreign invasion." In the end, Adams decided that the long-term threat, which wise policy might actually transform into an "extension of national power and security," was preferable to the immediate danger of

"Louisiana and the mouths of the Mississippi in the possession of France."[22]

Adams joined with the Republicans in supporting the treaty, but soon departed from them over the need for a constitutional amendment. Immediately after learning of the purchase, Jefferson and other Republican policymakers had recognized that nothing in the Constitution explicitly permitted the federal government to purchase territories and incorporate them into the union. Adams had no problem with the purchase itself. "The power *to make trea-ties*," he later explained, was *"without limitation,"* covering "whatever [might] form the subject of *treaties* between sovereign and independent nations." He did consider it unconstitutional, and unrepublican, for the United States to attempt to govern the people of Louisiana without their consent. In Adams's view, Congress could not even think of legislating for the people of Louisiana without an amendment to the Constitution authorizing it to make laws for them, as well as to extend to them the rights of other citizens and, eventually, to incorporate them into the union. Adams discussed his proposed amendment with the secretary of state before submitting it to the Senate, but Madison saw it as "too comprehensive" and argued for a much simpler statement that "'Louisiana is hereby admitted into this Union.'" Adams's amendment failed with just three votes in its favor. For the remainder of the session, he voted against the Republicans on all bills concerning the governance of Louisiana, believing that their effect was "to invest the President with all the absolute powers of a Spanish monarch over a Spanish colony."[23]

The Louisiana Purchase thus called on Adams to think, once more, about the special nature of policymaking for a republican union. The completion of the purchase seemed essential for the preservation of the union, at least once the treaty with France had been signed. Accordingly, Adams's "voice and opinion were *in favor* of the acquisition of Louisiana, and of the ratification of the treaty by which it was acquired," despite the opposition of his Federalist colleagues. At the same time, the treaty itself seemed to violate the basic "principle of our national independence"—the republican conviction that *"no people has the right to make laws for another people without their consent."* In order to preserve this principle, Adams offered a constitutional amendment and, after its defeat, voted against the Republicans as they legislated for the new territory. With his handling of the Louisiana Purchase, Adams showed what would become increasingly clear over the next quarter century of his life: he would support any policy that promised to strengthen the union and fell within the limits of the Constitution regardless of who originated or supported it. As would remain the case throughout his life, such behavior frustrated his nominal political allies, in this case New England Federalists. One Bostonian likened Adams to "a Kite without a Tail" that would "be impelled by every eddy Wind" and "pitch on one side and on the other." Committed "to shew[ing] his independence," Adams could not be relied upon to unite with the other Federalists in Congress even when he agreed with their "leading principles of Action."[24]

The ideas and views that Adams absorbed and adopted by the time of his fortieth birthday in July 1807 shaped his personality and his policymaking for the rest of his life. Between 1767 and 1787, he had learned, primarily from his parents, the principles and values of an educated, Christian, republican gentleman. Between 1787 and 1807, he had learned, largely from his own observations and experiences, the logic and limits of a federal, republican union. He expected the federal government to do much for the people, in keeping with its duty to improve society. But he also realized "that *every* public measure of great importance [would], in some degree, differently affect the partial interests and feelings of the different parts of the nation." Accordingly, he insisted that all Americans needed to accept that they shared "a deep a permanent and a paramount interest in *Union*." And he believed that it was the principal task of the federal government "to reconcile [any] conflicting interests." Policymakers, in Adams's thinking, needed to work actively to improve the lives of the people and to cement the bonds of the union.[25]

Notes

1. Abigail Adams to John Quincy Adams (hereafter JQA), November 20, 1783, *Adams Family Correspondence*, ed. L. H. Butterfield et al., 6 vols. to date (Cambridge, Mass., 1963–), 5:274 (hereafter *Correspondence*).

2. John Adams to Abigail Adams, April 15, 1776, ibid., 1:384; Abigail Adams to JQA, March 20, 1780, ibid., 3:310.

3. John Adams to JQA, March 16, 1777, ibid., 2:177–78.

4. John Adams to JQA, December 28, 1780, ibid., 4:56; John Adams to Abigail Adams, April 14, 1776, ibid., 1:382.

5. Abigail Adams to John Adams, November 11, 1783, ibid., 5:268; JQA to Abigail Adams, December 30, 1786, *Writings of John Quincy Adams*, ed. Worthington Chauncey Ford, 7 vols. (New York, 1913–1917), 1:29 (hereafter *Writings*).

6. John Adams to Abigail Adams, [May 12, 1780], *Correspondence*, 3:342.

7. JQA, "Upon the importance and necessity of public faith, to the well-being of a Community," July 18, 1787, *Diary of John Quincy Adams,* ed. David Grayson Allen et al., 2 vols. to date (Cambridge, Mass., 1981–), 2:262; JQA, diary entry, October 12, 1787, ibid., 302–3; JQA, diary entry, February 7, 1788, ibid., 357.

8. JQA, "Columbus II," [December 4, 1793], *Writings,* 1:160.

9. JQA to John Adams, April 12, 1794, Adams Papers, Massachusetts Historical Society, Boston (microfilm), reel 377; John Adams to JQA, April 23, 1794, ibid.; JQA to John Adams, May 26, 1794, ibid.; JQA, diary entry, [June 10, 1794], *Memoirs of John Quincy Adams: Comprising Portions of His Diary from 1795 to 1848,* ed. Charles Francis Adams, 12 vols. (Philadelphia, 1874–1877), 1:32 (hereafter *Memoirs*).

10. JQA to John Adams, January 14, 1797, *Writings,* 2:88.

11. JQA to Thomas Boylston Adams, February 14, 1801, ibid., 501; JQA to Charles Adams, June 9, 1796, ibid., 1:494.

12. JQA to Thomas Boylston Adams, February 14, 1801, ibid., 2:500–2.

13. JQA to John Adams, January 5, 1794, ibid., 1:178.

14. JQA to George Washington, February 11, 1797, ibid., 2:119, 120; JQA to Thomas Boylston Adams, December 3, 1800, ibid., 485. Adams's writings and Washington's address are closely compared in Samuel Flagg Bemis, "John Quincy Adams and George Washington," *Proceedings of the Massachusetts Historical Society* 67 (October 1941–May 1944): 365–84.

15. JQA, "Marcellus II," [May 4, 1793], *Writings,* 1:139; JQA, "Marcellus I," [April 24, 1793], ibid., 137.

16. JQA to William Vans Murray, July 22, 1798, ibid., 2:343–44; JQA to John Adams, June 24, 1796, ibid., 1:501; JQA to William Vans Murray, July 7, 1798, ibid., 2:335.

17. JQA to John Adams, April 3, 1797, ibid., 2:157; JQA to Thomas Boylston Adams, December 3, 1800, ibid., 484.

18. JQA, diary entry, January 28, 1802, *Memoirs,* 1:249.

19. JQA to William Vans Murray, April 7, 1801, *Writings,* 2:525, 526; JQA to Rufus King, October 8, 1802, ibid., 3:9.

20. JQA to William Vans Murray, April 7, 1801, ibid., 2:526.

21. JQA, speech of November 3, 1803, *Annals of Congress,* 8th Cong., 1st sess., 68; JQA, "Publius Valerius III," [October 30, 1804], *Writings,* 3:59.

22. John Breckinridge, speech of November 3, 1803, *Annals of Congress,* 8th Cong., 1st sess., 64–65; JQA, speech of November 3, 1803, ibid., 68; JQA, "Reply to the Appeal of the Massachusetts Federalists," [Spring 1829], *Documents Relating to New-England Federalism, 1800–1815,* ed. Henry Adams (Boston, 1877), 148 (hereafter *Documents*).

23. JQA to the Freeholders of Washington, Wythe, Grayson, Russell, Tazewell, Lee and Scott Counties, Virginia, December 28, 1822, *Writings,* 7:341; JQA, "Reply to the Appeal of the Massachusetts Federalists," [Spring 1829], *Documents,* 157; JQA to the Freeholders of Washington, Wythe, Grayson, Russell, Tazewell, Lee and Scott Counties, Virginia, December 28, 1822, *Writings,* 7:346.

24. JQA to the Freeholders of Washington, Wythe, Grayson, Russell, Tazewell, Lee and Scott Counties, Virginia, December 28, 1822, *Writings,* 7:341; JQA, "Notes of Speech on Motion," [ca. January 1804], ibid., 3:30, 29; Stephen Higginson to Timothy Pickering, February 15, 1804, in J. Franklin Jameson, ed., "Letters of Stephen Higginson, 1783–1804," in *An-*

nual Report of the American Historical Association for the Year 1896 (Washington, D.C., 1897), 839, 840.

25. JQA, [notes for speech on] "Proposed Amendment to the Constitution on Representation," [December 1804], *Writings*, 3:87, 88.

2

The Storms of War and Peace

1807–1817

"The really important period of my life," Secretary of State John Quincy Adams reflected in the spring of 1820, "began with the British attack upon our Chesapeake frigate, in the summer of 1807." Much happened to Adams even in just the ten years between the *Chesapeake* affair of June 1807 and his departure from Great Britain to take charge of the State Department in June 1817. And much happened to the country in this decade, as well. While the United States suffered through years of commercial restrictions, offensive and defensive war, and uneasy peace, Adams changed his political party, lost his Senate seat, accepted "honorable exile" in Europe as the minister to Russia, helped to negotiate the end of the War of 1812, and served as the minister to Great Britain. The events of these years, national and personal, had a profound impact upon Adams's views, helping to reinforce his existing concerns and shape his future goals as, first, secretary of state and, later, president. He closely watched the American people and the federal government as they struggled with French and British attacks on American trade, the Embargo, the gradual descent into war, and the War of 1812 itself. With the end of the war, he searched for the lessons of these struggles and tried to apply them to policymaking.[1]

Adams understood the problems of these years in a way that was increasingly uncommon among his contemporaries. His thinking remained true to the logic of the Founders, accepting the role of the federal union in securing the goals of the Revolution and the impact of republican principles on policymaking. He still viewed the

union as dangerously fragile. Under the strains of commercial re-
striction and war between 1807 and 1815, the conflicting interests
of its different sections had almost snapped the weak cords that
bound the union together. To Adams, it seemed more important
than ever before for policymakers to commit themselves to strengthening these bonds and shielding the union from new dangers.
Adams, along with a number of emerging Republican leaders, decided that neither the Federalist program of consolidating the union
into a single political entity nor the Republican program of dis-
persing energy from the center to the states and the people could
accomplish these goals. To meet new internal and external challenges, Adams called for using the powers of the federal government to the full extent allowed by the Constitution. This more
energetic government would follow "two political principles" that
he considered "best suited to the interests and the duties of this
country." "*UNION*" would direct "its internal concerns," while
"*INDEPENDENCE*" would guide "its intercourse with foreign nations." These principles usually seemed inseparable to Adams. He
insisted that the duties of the federal government encompassed
foreign and domestic threats to the union, internal and external
threats to independence.[2]

~

Like many statesmen in the late 1810s and early 1820s, Adams
drew lessons for future policymaking from the difficulties of the
federal government between 1807 and 1815. He experienced these
problems directly in the case of the Embargo and indirectly in the
case of the War of 1812, but they appeared very similar. As a senator, Adams debated the appropriate response to British and French
attacks on American commerce and the *Chesapeake* affair and voted
in favor of the Embargo. As a resident of Boston, he saw the Embargo virulently opposed and successfully violated. Soon after the
repeal of the Embargo, he left for Europe, where he served, first, as
the minister to Russia and, later, as one of the peace commissioners
at Ghent. Between the summer of 1809 and the spring of 1815, as
the United States moved toward and entered into a war with Great
Britain, Adams relied upon official correspondence, newspapers,
and letters from friends and family to provide the information that
fueled his fears. His firsthand experience of the Embargo colored
his interpretation of this new information. Having seen for himself
the fragility of the union and the weakness of the federal govern-

ment between 1807 and 1809, Adams could easily imagine the renewed problems of the war years between 1812 and 1815.

In the years after the Louisiana Purchase, Adams continued to
chart an independent course in the Senate. He acted with his Federalist colleagues on many issues. But he increasingly joined the
administration and its Republican supporters on issues related to
British and French restrictions on American neutral trade. In the
spring of 1806, when President Thomas Jefferson requested a non-
importation act aimed at selected British goods as a way to pressure Great Britain into relaxing its restrictions, Adams was the only
Federalist in either house of Congress to vote for it. A year later,
Adams also backed the president when he decided against even
submitting to the Senate a treaty that James Monroe and William
Pinkney had signed with Great Britain, which neither addressed
the problem of impressment nor resolved the dispute over blockades. Then, in June 1807, the British ship *Leopard* fired upon the
American ship *Chesapeake* off the coast of Virginia after the American commander refused to return alleged deserters from the British navy. Three men died, eighteen were wounded, and, after the
Chesapeake surrendered, four were taken away as deserters. In Boston, Adams suggested that the Federalists call a special town meeting to protest this outrage against the American flag and support
the administration, whatever its response. When Federalist leaders declined, he attended a Republican meeting and served on the
committee that drafted its resolutions. Federalists soon charged
Adams with "apostasy" from the party. But, in Adams's thinking,
it was not so much that he had deserted his party colleagues as
that "they [had] deserted their country."[3]

When the Senate met in October 1807, Adams moved even closer
to the administration position and even further from his nominal
colleagues. The initial war fever of the *Chesapeake* affair had eased,
leaving the administration with the freedom to decide its course.
Jefferson had already ordered British warships out of American
ports; Adams chaired the Senate committee that drafted a bill con-
firming this step. Jefferson had also demanded that the British cabinet disavow the actions of the *Leopard*, return the impressed
deserters, and end all impressment of American sailors. While
awaiting its response, the administration learned that the British
cabinet planned to announce additional restrictions on American
commerce. Fearing that new seizures of American ships would produce war and hoping that American pressure on British commerce
could bring relief, the president called on Congress to pass an

embargo in December 1807. Initially, the Embargo banned all maritime exports of American produce and all sailings of American ships except in the coastal trade between American ports; within a few months, it had been expanded to include overland trade into British and Spanish colonies. His diplomatic experience fully recognized by the Republican majority, Adams, once again, served on the committee that discussed Jefferson's request and provided the one Federalist vote in favor of the bill. Within ten days of voting for the Embargo, Adams acknowledged that, as a result of his pro-administration course, "[his] political prospects [were] declining." In May 1808, the Federalist-dominated Massachusetts legislature confirmed this analysis by prematurely selecting his replacement. In response, Adams resigned his Senate seat.[4]

Even though Adams voted for the Embargo in December 1807, he expected something vastly different from what the administration actually implemented over the next fourteen months. He supported the Embargo as the best way to preserve the peace and the union. He certainly viewed it as a way to counter British impressment, the threat of a sudden British attack on American shipping, and the recent British and French decrees about neutral rights. It would reduce the danger of war, he explained, by "diminish[ing] the temptations and opportunities of the enemy to commence war against us." But he also voted for the Embargo because opposing the administration on this important question seemed certain to endanger the union, making either a civil war or New England's secession likely. Nonetheless, Adams recognized that the policy would be "necessarily distressing to ourselves." He expected a temporary suspension of trade only, considering a total embargo lasting "six or twelve months" to be utterly impracticable "in a great commercial country." Even a brief embargo would serve as a test of "how far the Government might calculate upon the support of the people for the maintenance of their own rights." If they refused to accept the sacrifices required by the Embargo, Adams calculated, both the public and the policymakers would see the need to arrange terms with the European belligerents rather than pressing the dispute to the greater extremity of war.[5]

The Embargo brought none of the desired relief from British or French restrictions on American commerce, but it produced an alarming level of popular dissatisfaction. Opposition to the Embargo took a variety of forms in the country, in general, and in Massachusetts, in particular. Adams duly noted all of them. Merchants and sailors subverted the law by using permits for the coastal trade to ship goods to British Canada, sailing without any permit, trading with foreign ships offshore, and suborning customs officials. As jurors, a sympathetic public nullified the law by refusing to hand down guilty verdicts in embargo cases. Federalist lawyers attempted to have both the state and federal courts declare the Embargo unconstitutional. Federalist editors and politicians worked to mobilize public opinion in favor of a repeal of the Embargo. The Embargo, Adams reflected, eroded the support of the administration's New England "friends" and became a powerful "engine in the hands of" its Federalist opponents. As the opposition to the Embargo grew during the summer and fall of 1808, he saw disturbing evidence that leading Federalists viewed a division of the union as the only way to restore New England's commerce. They seemed committed to building public support for state efforts to counteract or repeal the Embargo. Such "an organized insurrection against the national government by State authority" Adams found alarming, as it was in this way "that the project of disunion [could] alone be accomplished."[6]

The administration's increasingly strict efforts to curtail trade, it seemed to Adams, only provided its opponents with new grounds for attacks. While the widespread violations sapped the coercive potential of the policy, they also demonstrated the inability of the federal government to enforce an unpopular law. Administration proposals to tighten the Embargo as it entered its twelfth month alarmed Adams. In order to redress the shortage of federal officials on the northern and southern borders, Jefferson and Secretary of the Treasury Albert Gallatin wanted Congress to empower the state governments to enforce the Embargo. Such a step seemed likely to prove disastrous in Massachusetts. The new enforcement law, Adams predicted, "will not be executed in this quarter of the Union by the ordinary process." It placed great reliance on the people and on state officials when there could be little doubt that "juries, judges and militia [would] all fail to perform their parts." The new measures, Adams concluded, "will infallibly meet with direct resistance, which nothing but force will overpower." A tougher enforcement law would merely play into the hands of the most radical Federalists, who saw the use of federal force against a state government as an issue that would win popular backing for their disunionist schemes. In a series of letters to his friends in Congress during the winter of 1808–1809, Adams called for relaxing rather than strengthening the Embargo. He believed that a nonintercourse act that prohibited all trade—both exports and imports—but only with Great

Britain and France might increase the risk of a foreign war, but it would "diminish the dangers of internal commotion."[7]

In the final days of the Jefferson administration in March 1809, the Republican majority in Congress repealed the Embargo and passed the Non-Intercourse Act; in the first days of the new administration, President James Madison appointed Adams minister to Russia. Adams certainly approved of the nation's new stance in its dispute with Great Britain and France. He was less certain about his own new station. There was little question that the mission to Russia was important. With nearly all of Europe controlled by either Napoleonic France or Great Britain and subject to their commercial restrictions, Russia offered the most important European market for American produce and remained the last potential European advocate of neutral rights. Still, the mission appeared "stormy and dangerous" to Adams, with only an "unpromising prospect" of success. Since resigning his Senate seat, he had enjoyed practicing law and teaching rhetoric and oratory at Harvard. His family included a wife and three sons—the oldest seven and the youngest one—as well as two elderly parents; they would all be better served, he thought, by his remaining in the United States. But he strongly felt his duty to his country and the new president, who, he was "perfectly convinced," was committed to "the welfare of this whole Union." He also had at least "the vague *hope* of rendering to [his] country some important service." Finally, he could draw some "satisfaction" from the knowledge that his new mission would distance him, "at least for a time, and with honor, from . . . the most virulent and unrelenting persecution" by his Federalist neighbors.[8]

Over the next few years, Adams found Czar Alexander I sympathetic to the American position between Great Britain and France and attached to the American trade with Russia. But there was little that either Adams and the czar in Europe or Madison and Congress in the United States could do to ease French and British pressure on American commerce. Between the spring of 1809 and the summer of 1811, policymakers experimented with a number of forms of economic coercion aimed at Great Britain or France or both. None of these steps brought the relief that they sought; all of them inflamed the problems seen during the Embargo as the people violated the laws, the parties grew increasingly hostile and divided, and the federal government proved unable to enforce its will. By the summer of 1811, Madison reluctantly concluded that a war with Great Britain over neutral rights and impressment offered the only way to save the union and redeem the federal government. He called on Congress to prepare for war that fall and quietly helped to guide it toward a declaration of war the following June. Madison and most Republicans entered the war with high hopes. They expected to conquer British Canada easily and to use it as leverage to force the British cabinet to end its restrictions on American trade and its impressment of American sailors. But events did not unfold as hoped. By November 1812, Adams could accurately describe his country's military efforts as a "burlesque upon War," and things only grew worse from there.[9]

In the months before the declaration of war, Adams predicted many of the problems that the government would face in waging it. Recent events from the embargo years, including the disunionism of New England Federalists and the ineffectiveness of the federal government, shaped his expectations about the impending war. He foresaw the difficulties in enlisting men, raising revenue, and mobilizing resources. He recognized that the United States possessed ample resources for the war, but also understood that "the most formidable difficulty [would] be to bring them forth." And he lamented the federal government's failure to prepare more adequately for war in the years after the *Chesapeake* affair. The actions of the most radical Federalists during the Embargo, moreover, had convinced Adams that a war with Great Britain would exacerbate existing sectional and partisanal tensions within the United States. Writing to his father in July 1811, he predicted that such a war would produce, as "one of its earliest effects[,] . . . a struggle for the division of the states." There could be no doubt, he warned, that it would lead to sweeping "changes of popular sentiments[,] of administrations, and perhaps of constitutions in our country." These considerations prompted Adams to favor continued preparation and negotiation rather than war as late as the spring of 1812.[10]

The course of the War of 1812 itself blasted any of Adams's lingering hopes that the federal government could find a way to marshal the nation's "latent energy" and overcome its internal divisions. He applauded the early successes of the navy, but moaned that the initial failures of the army against Canada "[made] us the scorn and laughter of all Europe." Since "our means of taking [Canada were] so ample and unquestionable," the failure to conquer it could only result from the absence of the republican virtue of self-sacrifice that still seemed essential to independence. During the first two years of the war, letters and papers from the United States regularly reinforced Adams's sense that the federal government seemed incapable of guiding the people and the military to a victory. At the same time, he recognized that the Federalists were laboring to obstruct the war effort. Though consistent with their history of trying to frustrate Republican policies, their tactics jeopardized the very independence of the United States. The refusal of New England's Federalist governors to call out their state militias for federal service especially alarmed Adams. He worried that the Federalists seemed willing "to prostrate the nation at the feet of a foreign enemy, for the sake of obtaining a triumph over a rival party." Adams calculated that the opposition in New England only inspired the British cabinet—whose "real object in the present war [was] the dismemberment of the American Union"— to prolong a war that the Federalists were trying to end.[11]

But, in Adams's view, the difficulties of the war's first two years paled in comparison to the shocking developments of its final six months. He expected that the influx of British troops after the defeat of France in the spring of 1814 "*must* in the first instance make powerful impressions." Still, the force of these "impressions," particularly the destruction of Washington in August, came as a shock. More surprising was the news that reached Adams and the other peace commissioners at Ghent, Belgium, during the fall of 1814 showing the failure of the federal government to meet this shock energetically. By mid-November, Adams retained little faith in either the "feeble and penurious government" or the people, "half" of whom were "sold by their prejudice and their ignorance to our enemy." Two weeks later, Adams received further evidence of domestic divisions in the form of reports of the planned Hartford Convention of the New England states. Adams believed that, whatever their avowed intentions, the Federalists sought the dissolution of the union as the route to power. With the peace talks ongoing, the news of their "mad and wicked project of national suicide" seemed certain to encourage British obstinacy and result in a longer war. The delays of trans-Atlantic communications and the secrecy of the convention itself meant that it was not until after completing the peace treaty that Adams fully understood the challenge of the Hartford Convention and the paralysis of the federal government in the last months of the war.[12]

At Ghent, Adams and the other American commissioners— Henry Clay, Albert Gallatin, Jonathan Russell, and the Federalist James A. Bayard—faced a difficult situation. The redeployment of thousands of seasoned British soldiers had transformed the War of 1812 from an offensive one—invading Canada—to a defensive one

—protecting American cities and frontiers. A British invasion of the Gulf Coast aimed at New Orleans, moreover, seemed imminent. Conversely, the federal government was still reeling from the fall of the capital as neither Congress nor the states would entrust the administration with the manpower and resources needed either to defend the country or to invade Canada. And the New England Federalists, at least, appeared poised to divide the union and seek a separate peace with Great Britain. Making matters worse for the American delegation were some early conflicts among its members. Though selected with an eye to representing most of the sectional and political perspectives in the United States, their differences tended to be personal rather than political. The hardworking Adams believed that his colleagues wasted too much time and money on parties, concerts, balls, plays, cards, and billiards; they considered him hardheaded and aloof. It took some time, moreover, for Adams, who nominally headed the commission, and Gallatin, who commanded more respect from its other members, to sort out their respective roles.

At issue in the negotiations were not only the old questions about neutral rights and impressment that had led to the war but also a pair of new demands by the British. The British called for a revision of the boundary between Canada and the United States and the creation of a "neutral zone" for the northwestern Indians south of the Great Lakes. They also insisted that the outbreak of war had terminated the American right to fish off Canada—an issue of tremendous importance to New Englanders and, thus, to Adams. Despite the weakness of the American position, Adams and his colleagues rebuffed or deflected the new demands. They succeeded, in part, by reminding the British of the inherent and acknowledged weakness of republican governments. As Adams insisted, trying to stop white encroachment upon Indian lands by law or by force would be "opposing a feather to a torrent." A republican government simply could not check the land hunger of the growing American population, he argued, whatever the terms of the treaty signed with Great Britain. In the end, the Treaty of Ghent said nothing about an Indian barrier state and left the Canadian-American boundary unchanged. Nor did it say anything about neutral rights or impressment, for that matter. Preoccupied by European affairs and disappointed by news of recent defeats in upstate New York and Baltimore, Maryland, the British agreed to a treaty that merely ended the war and restored the status quo ante bellum.[13]

For Adams, the years of crisis between the *Chesapeake* affair of the summer of 1807 and the ratification of the Treaty of Ghent in the spring of 1815 served to confirm and deepen preexisting ideas and concerns. The inability of the federal government to enforce its will upon the people and the states highlighted, once again, the fundamental differences between the United States's nontraditional republican government and Europe's traditional monarchical goverments. The rise of disunionist sentiment in New England called forth from Adams renewed statements of his commitment to union and his adherence to the thinking of the Founders. Responding to the first signs of Federalist separatism in the spring of 1809, for example, he warned that disunion would bring "in its train an endless perspective of unextinguishable war." "Union is peace," Adams insisted, "and peace is liberty." As he flatly explained to his father in the fall of 1811, without union "there [could] be no good government among the people of North America." The newly demonstrated weakness of the federal government and fragility of the federal union seemed to demand a quick, but acceptable, end to the war in 1814 and an immediate, and dramatic, change in policy after the peace.[14]

~

Writing from his new diplomatic post as minister to Great Britain in May 1816, Adams reflected that the American people seemed "inclined to be rather more proud than they [had] reason of the war from which they [had] so recently emerged." In his view, they "look[ed] too intently to their triumphs, and turn[ed] their eyes too lightly away from their disasters." Between the signing of the peace treaty in December 1814 and his departure from Europe to take charge of the State Department in June 1817, Adams filled his official and personal letters with his analysis of the lessons of recent years and of the state of international politics. Worried that the United States would soon find itself at war again, he argued that policymakers and the public had to act energetically to strengthen the union and its government. He emerged from the crisis deeply impressed with two ideas. First, he believed that the United States needed "some years of peace" in which policymakers could "seek and devise remedies for the evils which we [had] experienced in the late war," including not only expanding the army and navy but also encouraging "domestic manufactures" and stabilizing the financial system. Second, he insisted that the federal government needed to act to the full extent of its constitutional powers to cement the bonds of union. Federal energy would attach the nation's far-flung citizens to the union, exert the gravity needed to keep the states in their proper orbit, and defend the union in a dangerous world. Only by using the full powers of the government could policymakers ensure that the Constitution fulfilled its purpose of establishing a union of the states that would secure the goals of the Revolution.[15]

As the minister to Great Britain following the War of 1812, Adams served two crucial functions. His meetings with Viscount Castlereagh, the British foreign minister, helped to ease recent tensions. Adams well understood that, under the Treaty of Ghent, "nothing was adjusted, nothing was settled." With both Adams and Castlereagh anxious for a period of peace, some important issues were resolved during Adams's two years in London. In July 1815, Adams, Gallatin, and Clay concluded a commercial treaty in which each party agreed to treat the other's ships, goods, and citizens or subjects the same as its own in its ports. It also prohibited discriminatory duties on either exports or imports. In early 1816, Adams began discussions with Castlereagh regarding limiting naval armaments on the Great Lakes. These talks eventually resulted in the Rush-Bagot Agreement of April 1817, perhaps the first agreement of its kind in history. But these agreements left many issues either unresolved or unaddressed. The Convention of 1815 applied only to the British Isles, with less favorable terms for American trade in the British East Indies and no provision for American trade in the British West Indies. The Rush-Bagot Agreement may have prevented a naval arms race, but it did not eliminate naval vessels from the lakes entirely. And Adams made no headway at all on neutral rights or impressment.[16]

More important, perhaps, Adams regularly sent President Madison and Secretary of State James Monroe informed and extended assessments of the state of European politics from London. His analysis of conditions throughout the continent and in Great Britain after more than two decades of almost constant warfare reinforced his own and the administration's conviction that the postwar world was a very dangerous place for the United States. He concluded that the instability within each nation and the hostility between them would create pressures that Europe's balance-of-power system could not peacefully contain. A new European war seemed inevitable. Adams could imagine a number of ways in which this volatile international situation threatened the United States.

Considering peace essential, Madison, Monroe, and Adams shaped their postwar policies with this sense of danger foremost in their thinking.

The quarter century of European war that ended with Napoleon's defeat at Waterloo in June 1815 dramatically reshaped Adams's thinking about international relations. As a young man, he had partaken of the Enlightenment's confidence that the law of nations and the balance of power would bring peace, more liberal government, and moral improvement to Europe. By 1801, however, he rejected this view as a part of "the flood of philosophy which poured upon that self-conceited dupe, the eighteenth century." Over the next fifteen years, he grew increasingly convinced of the irrationality and immorality of European diplomacy. "Nine times out of ten," Adams insisted, "if a measure is clearly for the interest of the nation, the government will reject it." Passions, not interests, and power, not morals, seemed to drive European diplomacy. The suppression of the French Revolution by force, moreover, entrenched absolutist rule throughout Europe and created explosive pressures within each nation. New wars might offer the only way for Europe's monarchs to ease this pressure. "In Peace," Adams reasoned, the European powers "would find their destruction" because they would have no way to vent "those deadly humours of National Corruption, which if allowed to be thrown back upon their own vitals would produce speedy and inevitable death." It was not just internal forces that pointed toward new wars, however. There were also jealousies among the victors and a desire for revenge on the part of the vanquished left over from the recent war. Adams could find nothing in the new state system devised by the Congress of Vienna that might preserve the peace. "The foundation upon which the present peace of Europe is professedly laid," he explained in November 1815, "is in its nature weak and treacherous."[17]

This image of a European political system stripped of reason and morality, propelled toward war by forces within each state, and unrestrained by the balance of power bore heavily on Adams's thinking in the postwar era. He saw grave dangers to the United States in the condition of post-Napoleonic Europe. With each new development, he reassessed how long a new war could be postponed. In time, Adams simply concluded that "the tranquillity of Europe [was] precarious [and] liable to many sudden changes and great convulsions." None of these changes, he decided, "would give us more security than we now enjoy against the bursting of another storm upon ourselves." Adams believed that the threats to the United States came from three sources. He worried that one or more European powers would initiate a war with the United States intentionally, either because it embodied the republican principles that threatened their own governments or because it could provide an easy target for a war that was "indispensably necessary to save [their] nation from internal convulsions." At the same time, he expected that a new general war in Europe would produce the same kinds of collisions over neutral rights and impressment between the United States and the belligerents that had led to war in 1812. Finally, Adams feared that, given the volatility within Europe and throughout Spain's New World empire, a new war might emerge as the final, and unpredictable, link in a chain of events that began with a minor collision. "With all those combustible materials," Adams reflected in October 1815, "we shall be favored in full measure by heaven, if we succeed in preserving peace for a series of years."[18]

At the center of all of Adams's postwar security concerns stood Great Britain. More than any other European power, Great Britain seemed likely to enter into a war with the United States deliberately. The British public, Adams observed, despised the United States for declaring war in 1812 and then winning a number of naval victories. The cabinet was less hostile. But, whether it wanted peace or not, it might "plunge the nation headlong into a war with us" because a new Anglo-American war would be popular and might be the only way to ease domestic pressures. Similarly, Great Britain would present the greatest problems in the event of a renewed general war in Europe, just as it had before 1812. Any European war would almost certainly involve the British, who would try to use their navy to interdict trade to their enemies. Since the Treaty of Ghent had not resolved the controveries over neutral rights and impressment, Adams expected "that the object of the last war must perhaps, and not improbably, be fought for again." Finally, it was easy to imagine a war with Great Britain arising over even a relatively minor issue. The combination of commerce, colonies, and alliances gave the British worldwide interests. With their colonies in Canada, alliance with Spain, and ties to Indians across North America, the British considered themselves deeply interested around, and within, the United States's borders. Long after the Treaty of Ghent restored peace between the two nations, Adams worried that old conflicts and new collisions might bring another war.[19]

The course of a quarter century of war and the nature of the peace that ended it convinced Adams, like many policymakers, that the United States would face new dangers in the postwar world. A planned attack on the United States, a general war in Europe, or even an accidental rupture, moreover, would strain bonds of union that Adams still considered perilously weak. European statesmen, he believed, also understood the union's contribution to American strength and its precariousness after the War of 1812. Worried that the United States would "become a very dangerous member of the society of nations" as its wealth and population grew, they hoped that the union would dissolve "into two or more nations in opposition against one another." Adams calculated that, in a war against the United States, any European power would work deliberately to break apart the union. Given the hostility, volatility, and unpredictability of the world, he insisted that the United States needed to remain entirely aloof from European affairs and avoid unnecessarily risky behavior of its own in order to shield the weak union from new dangers. "The contemplation of our external relations," he further argued in the summer of 1816, "makes me specially anxious to strengthen our national government."[20]

Adams's understanding of the crisis that faced the union and its government between 1807 and 1815 only confirmed his concerns about a weak union and his desire for an energetic government. Where most postwar policymakers accepted that increased federal energy was needed to bolster the nation's military preparedness, Adams—along with Henry Clay, John C. Calhoun, and other members of a rising generation of policymakers—insisted that redoubled federal efforts were needed to strengthen the union's weak ties. Confronting evidence of the disunionism of Massachusetts Federalists in the spring of 1809, Adams had restated his belief that it was "the most sacred duty" of American policymakers "to inculcate such principles and such sentiments, as have a natural tendency to give duration and stability to [the] Union." After the War of 1812, this continuing concern for the union separated Adams from leading Republicans such as Madison and Monroe, who seemed confident of its strength and permanence. It did not, however, mark a return to the Federalist program of the 1790s. Adams viewed himself as firmly grounded in Republican thought; he saw the Constitution as a limited grant of powers, accepted the need for vigorous state governments, and trusted the political and economic choices of the mass of the people. Yet he worried that, since 1801, the Republicans had abdicated some of the legitimate powers and abandoned some of the necessary duties of the federal government. After 1815, Adams supported various policies, often with Republican antecedents, to redress the fragility of the union and the infirmity of the government.[21]

Even after the disasters of the War of 1812, Adams thought that the only real danger to the United States lay in a division of the union. "Disunion," he insisted in 1816, "is the only fatal mischief which in the natural course of events can for many ages befall our country." If the union held, Americans could expect to be "the most populous and most powerful people ever combined under one social compact" and to possess "a nation, coextensive with the North American continent." If the union dissolved, they would instead find themselves divided into "an endless multitude of little insignificant clans and tribes at eternal war with one another for a rock, or a fish pond, the sport and fable of European masters and oppressors." The crisis of recent years had heightened Adams's fears that the union could not hold. The limits on American commerce and the war with Great Britain had clearly shown that important interests—deriving from party loyalties, economic activities, and foreign sympathies—remained divided along sectional lines. Adams might publicly argue that "there [was] no real opposition of interests between any one part of this union and another." But too many people thought otherwise. Perhaps the gravest danger, in Adams's view, was that party leaders who were frustrated in their efforts to win national offices would play upon the common perception of conflicting sectional interests to gain control of at least a fragment of the union. Concerned about New England's Federalists in particular, he warned in early 1816 that "projects of severing the Union . . . were too deeply seated in the political systems, as well as in the views of personal ambition . . . , to be yet abandoned."[22]

Adams expected federal policymakers to take responsibility for strengthening the union by removing the ultimate sources of disunionism—the disparate interests of its different sections. The best security for the union, he believed, lay in an economic and social order that balanced and distributed the manufacturing, agricultural, and commercial sectors within a national market that included a healthy currency system. Such a "home market," as it was often called at the time, would create dependencies and connections between the different economic sectors and geographic sections. It was also expected to promote diversity by fostering locally integrated economies—of farmers, merchants, small- and medium-scale manufacturers, and professionals—in every section of the union. A vibrant home market would ease the pressures caused by commercial restrictions and blur the lines drawn by sectional interests, thus reducing the union's susceptibility to external pressures. A national bank, a system of roads and canals, a protective tariff, and the controlled sale of public lands all seemed essential to the development of this more complex economy. All of these steps, Adams argued, fell within the existing powers of the federal government. Leading Republicans disagreed. But it was their very constraint of federal power, promotion of states' rights, and call for strict construction that had weakened the union, in Adams's thinking. A postwar commitment to energetic federal action in the form of a new bank, internal improvements, higher tariffs, and new land policies could reverse the damage by creating an economic and social order that promoted union against internal and external strains.

Following the war, Adams sought policies that would increase not only the cohesiveness of the union but also the effectiveness of the federal government. Between 1807 and 1815, the limits of federal power and authority, even beyond the obvious inadequacies of the military, had plagued the government's efforts, first, to avoid war through economic coercion and, later, to wage war against Great Britain. Popular violations of trade restrictions, state obstruction of wartime measures, intergovernmental tensions between Congress and the administration, and partisan opposition to essential policies had combined to rob the government of its vitality. Just as he urged policymakers to energize the federal government internally by using all of its legitimate powers, Adams also sought ways to remove such external obstacles to federal energy. The ebbing of Federalist influence, particularly at the national level, eased one of his concerns, though he continued to worry that, in a republic, "the passions . . . [would] never suffer opinions for any length of time to harmonize." He focused his postwar efforts on promoting federal power and authority over the people and the states and asserting executive branch control over foreign relations. Such efforts, he hoped, would make it easier for federal policymakers to strengthen the union in times of peace and defend it in times of war.[23]

Adams tackled the obstacles to federal power and authority cautiously. Many of the government's difficulties, he realized, stemmed from the nation's most important values—political self-determination and economic freedom. In a republic, the expansive energies and productive efforts of the people could be managed only delicately, if at all. Like most Republicans, he saw these political and economic liberties as the basic source of American strength. While it might, on occasion, be necessary to enforce unpopular laws, the Embargo had convinced Adams of the problems, and even dangers, of trying to do so. He preferred to attach the people to the government not by overawing or overpowering them, but by showing them that it was the source of such benefits as a stable currency, improved transportation, and higher tariffs. Voluntary deference to federal authority, rather than compulsory obedience to federal power, appeared likely to derive from and contribute to new evidence of federal energy. In the same way, the imbalance of power that Adams saw between the federal and state governments had to be redressed within the parameters of the Constitution. Its distribution of powers seemed essential for preserving the union. The problems arose not from the Constitution itself, but from the failure of Virginia Republicans to maintain its careful distribution. Adams found the extent to which they had ceded federal powers to the states "politic enough for a citizen of the most powerful state in the union, but . . . good for nothing for the weaker states, and pernicious for the whole."[24]

For Adams, energizing the federal government also required easing the stalemating effect of conflicts between the executive and legislative branches, which had certainly crippled the war effort. He thought that on many issues the two branches should act as equals, on some issues, including internal improvements and tariffs, the legislature should take the lead, and on other issues, especially foreign relations, the executive should decide policy. In the early postwar period, Adams was pleased by the relative harmony with which the administration and Congress worked together to solve problems. With the president's messages outlining policies and Congress developing them in full, the federal government quickly enlarged the peacetime army and navy, funded frontier and coastal defenses, raised the tariff, and established the Second Bank of the United States. Despite the success of this process on these issues, Adams insisted on complete executive branch control over foreign relations. He traced the main obstacles to such control to "that error in our Constitution" that gave Congress the power to declare war. This initial "error" in the division of power, Adams believed, tended to encourage further congressional incursions upon the legitimate authority of the executive. Congressional interference, in any number of forms, prevented the president and secretary of state from bringing to bear upon foreign powers all of the diplomatic leverage that should have been available to them. As secretary of state beginning in the fall of 1817, Adams would clash repeatedly with Congress, particularly Speaker of the House Clay, over the Congress's role in foreign relations.[25]

Even as he worked to extend federal authority and power and to increase executive control after 1815, Adams further developed his talents at manipulating the federal government's weakness to the nation's diplomatic advantage. Over the course of the 1790s, he had recognized that the United States's republican government could never claim the control over its own citizens enjoyed by Europe's monarchies. He had regretted this reality initially and continued to do so, at times, during and after the War of 1812. But he had also learned its usefulness, as demonstrated by his role in deflecting British proposals for an Indian neutral zone during the Ghent negotiations. In March 1816, Adams applied this argument to a new issue. After the return of peace in Europe and the restoration of the Spanish king, Spanish diplomats in Madrid, Washington, and London angrily complained that, despite official claims of neutrality, Americans were actively assisting Spain's rebellious colonies by serving as privateers (seizing its merchant ships) and filibusters (invading its neighboring colonies) on their behalf. While Madison and Monroe tried to rebuff Spain's complaints and prevent such activities, Adams argued to the Spanish minister in London that the American republic simply could not be held to the same standards as the European monarchies. The United States lacked the "fortified cities," "corps of gendarmerie [police]," and power of arbitrary arrest that gave European powers "immediate [and] complete control over" their subjects. In Adams's view, as long as the activities were "neither . . . sanctioned nor connived at by the American government" and were combatted "according to the forms allowed by our Constitution," the United States had met its obligations as a neutral and Spain had no cause for complaint.[26]

In April 1817, Adams received word that the newly elected president, James Monroe, had named him secretary of state. This new position would afford him a greater opportunity to shape policies that reflected his concerns and views. He had emerged from the recent crisis impressed by the tenuousness of the union, the weakness of the government, and the dangers of the international system. Writing to his father in August 1816, he had captured the essence of his postwar thought: "My system of politics more and more inclines to strengthen the union and its government." Convinced that a new war was imminent and that neither the union nor its government could withstand it, he called for restraint abroad and vigor at home. After the War of 1812, as before, Adams had no doubt that "the first duty of an American statesman [was] to conciliate and unite" the "various and in some respects conflicting interests" of the different sections. At the same time, he expected federal energy to redress the imbalance of power and authority that favored the states and the people over the federal government. His views on this matter, he thought, were "directly the reverse" of those of many Republican policymakers who "rel[ied] principally upon the state governments." Without adopting the Federalist program of the 1790s, Adams insisted that increased federal energy was needed to shield the union from external and internal threats.[27]

~

In the decade between the *Chesapeake* affair and his return from London, developments at home and abroad reinforced for Adams the logic of the Founders. The Embargo and the War of 1812 had raised the specter of disunion, thus jeopardizing all of his hopes of national independence, republican government, commercial prosperity, and territorial expansion. A quarter century of war in Europe, moreover, had shown the volatility of international relations, thus suggesting the likelihood of new wars that would threaten American interests and union. To meet these internal and external dangers, Adams called for energetic measures by federal policymakers committed to strengthening the union and restoring federal authority and power. The United States, Adams stressed, needed to "persevere in the system of keeping aloof from all [Europe's] broils, and in that of consolidating and perpetuating our own Union." He never doubted that these two "systems"—avoiding European disputes and cementing American union—depended upon each other, demanding a single approach to policymaking rather than separate foreign and domestic policies.[28]

Notes

1. John Quincy Adams (hereafter JQA), diary entry, "Day" [May 1820], *Memoirs of John Quincy Adams: Comprising Portions of His Diary from 1795 to 1848*, ed. Charles Francis Adams, 12 vols. (Philadelphia, 1874–1877), 5:136 (hereafter *Memoirs*); Ezekial Bacon to JQA, June 29, 1809, *Writings of John Quincy Adams*, ed. Worthington Chauncey Ford, 7 vols. (New York, 1913–1917), 3:321 n.1 (hereafter *Writings*).

2. JQA to Skelton Jones, April 17, 1809, *Writings*, 3:300.

3. JQA, "Reply to the Appeal of the Massachusetts Federalists," [Spring 1829], *Documents Relating to New-England Federalism, 1800–1815*, ed. Henry Adams (Boston, 1877), 183 (hereafter *Documents*).

4. JQA, diary entry, "Day" [December 1807], *Memoirs*, 1:498.

5. JQA to James Sullivan, January 10, 1808, *Writings*, 3:186–87.

6. JQA to Ezekial Bacon, December 21, 1808, ibid., 278; JQA to Ezekial Bacon, November 17, 1808, ibid., 250–51.

7. JQA to Joseph Anderson, December 15, 1808, ibid., 271; JQA to Orchard Cook, December 8, 1808, ibid., 262.

8. JQA, diary entry, July 5, 1809, *Memoirs*, 1:549.

9. JQA to John Adams, November 5, 1812, Charles Francis Adams, ed., "Correspondence of John Quincy Adams, 1811–1814," *Proceedings of the American Antiquarian Society* new ser., 23 (April 1913): 123 (hereafter "Correspondence").

10. JQA to Benjamin Waterhouse, August 28, 1811, *Writings*, 4:197; JQA to John Adams, July 26, 1811, ibid., 147; JQA to Thomas Boylston Adams, July 31, 1811, ibid., 162.

11. JQA to Abigail Adams, March 30, 1812, ibid., 304; JQA to Abigail Adams, January 30, 1813, "Correspondence," 138; JQA to Thomas Boylston Adams, November 24, 1812, *Writings*, 4:407; JQA to Benjamin Waterhouse, August 11, 1813, ibid., 502; JQA to Abigail Adams, February 18, 1813, ibid., 435.

12. JQA to William Harris Crawford, August 29, 1814, *Writings*, 5:105; JQA to Levett Harris, November 15, 1814, ibid., 187; JQA to Louisa Catherine Adams, November 29, 1814, ibid., 219. Adams later discussed the Hartford Convention at great length in his "Reply to the Appeal of the Massachusetts Federalists," [Spring 1829], *Documents*, 107–329 passim.

13. JQA to James Monroe, September 5, 1814, *Writings*, 5:116.

14. [JQA], *American Principles: A Review of Works of Fisher Ames, Compiled by a Number of His Friends* (Boston, 1809), 37; JQA to John Adams, October 31, 1811, *Writings*, 4:267.

15. JQA to John Adams, May 29, 1816, *Writings*, 6:38; JQA to William Plumer, October 5, 1815, ibid., 5:400; JQA to Peter Paul Francis DeGrand, April 28, 1815, ibid., 314.

16. JQA to Joseph Hall, September 9, 1815, ibid., 5:372.

17. JQA to Thomas Boylston Adams, February 14, 1801, ibid., 2:500; JQA to Ezekial Bacon, December 21, 1808, ibid., 3:279; JQA to John Adams, November 5, 1812, "Correspondence," 124; JQA to John Thornton Kirkland, November 30, 1815, *Writings*, 5:431.

18. JQA to John Adams, August 1, 1816, *Writings*, 6:61; JQA to Abigail Adams, December 23, 1815, ibid., 5:454; JQA to William Plumer, October 5, 1815, ibid., 401.

19. JQA to John Adams, October 9, 1815, ibid., 5:410; JQA to Alexander Hill Everett, March 16, 1816, ibid., 537.

20. JQA to William Plumer, January 17, 1817, ibid., 6:143, 144; JQA to John Adams, August 1, 1816, ibid., 60.

21. [JQA], *American Principles*, 42–43.

22. JQA to Samuel Dexter, April 14, 1816, *Writings*, 6:15; JQA to Abigail Adams, June 30, 1811, ibid., 4:128; [JQA], *American Principles*, 36; JQA to Alexander Hill Everett, March 16, 1816, *Writings*, 5:538.

23. JQA to John Adams, October 5, 1817, *Writings*, 6:209.

24. JQA to John Adams, August 1, 1816, ibid., 60.

25. JQA, diary entry, December 30, 1817, *Memoirs*, 4:32.

26. JQA to James Monroe, March 30, 1816, *Writings*, 5:553.

27. JQA to John Adams, August 1, 1816, ibid., 6:60; JQA to Christopher Hughes, December 25, 1816, ibid., 129; JQA to John Adams, August 1, 1816, ibid., 60.

28. JQA to Joseph Hall, September 9, 1815, ibid., 5:376–77.

3

A Dangerous Neighborhood

1817–1821

Writing from London after hearing of James Monroe's election as president and before learning of his own appointment as secretary of state, John Quincy Adams recorded his sense of the important responsibilities facing the new administration. "It will be the great duty of [the incoming president], and of the Congress with which he is to cooperate," Adams suggested in early 1817, "to use diligently the days of peace to prepare the nation for other trials which are probably not far distant, and which sooner or later cannot fail to arise." This assertion might be restated as three interconnected propositions. First, after the War of 1812, peace seemed essential to the United States; but the volatile condition of Europe, the simmering revolutions in Spain's New World colonies, and, most alarmingly, the continuing tensions on the country's borders made this peace precarious. Second, postwar policymakers needed to use this period of peace, which they might be able to prolong, to prepare the nation for the next crisis. Third, their efforts should seek to strengthen the bonds of the union and to increase the authority of the federal government in order to ensure stability, prosperity, and security in the future. Throughout his tenure as secretary of state, but especially at the beginning, Adams analyzed developments in the United States, the New World, and Europe and devised policies to meet them with these propositions in mind.[1]

In his diary and correspondence, Adams initially expressed a great deal of anxiety about his ability "to justify [Monroe's] choice by active, efficient, and acceptable assistance to his administration, and the expectation of the public by solid and useful advice to my country." But his actions as secretary, from the very first, showed instead a confidence that, the more he assumed direction of the carrots and sticks of diplomacy, the better for the nation. By bringing the interactions of the American people and government with foreign powers more fully under the control of the federal government, in general, and the executive branch, in particular, Adams expected to improve the chances for preserving peace for the present and promoting commercial and territorial expansion in the future. In fact, the first term of Adams's service was marked by notable foreign policy successes, including not only four years of peace but also the Convention of 1818 with Great Britain and the Transcontinental Treaty with Spain. Ironically, however, these successes resulted more from the failure, or even the abandonment, of Adams's efforts to assert control over foreign relations than from his limited achievements in this area. Nor did these successes produce the results that Adams had expected. As a result of the sectional tensions and other problems generated by the Missouri Crisis and the Panic of 1819, the union seemed less secure and less stable in early 1821 than in early 1817. The final accounting of Adams's first term as secretary of state shows a mix of successes and failures.[2]

~

When Adams assumed control over the State Department in late September 1817, he had a very clear idea of his short-, medium-, and long-term goals. In the immediate future, Adams thought, the preeminent interest of the United States was to preserve a peace that seemed extremely fragile, especially given the conflicts and collisions between the United States and its immediate neighbors. By either resolving or postponing a resolution of these conflicts, Adams hoped to buy time in which the federal government could enhance the power and stability of the United States and he could increase his own control over American foreign relations. These medium-term steps would ultimately permit him, or his successors, to achieve the long-term goals of territorial and commercial expansion that Adams considered essential for a permanent union. For the most part, Monroe shared this thinking, as both the president and his secretary of state remained deeply impressed with the lessons of the War of 1812 and truly alarmed at the condition of the world around them. They frequently differed over tactical questions, but generally agreed upon the importance of immediate peace and future expansion.

For Monroe and Adams, what made the peace so precarious in the first years after the War of 1812 was the number, the extent, and the interconnectedness of the disputes between the United States and its British, Indian, and Spanish neighbors. "The relations with Spain," which "include[d] those with South America," "those with Great Britain, and Indian affairs," Adams noted midway through his first year in office, were "the points upon which important interests in this country are depending." In the postwar period, the United States disputed significant territorial, commercial, and diplomatic questions with each of these neighbors. A formal alliance between Great Britain and Spain and informal ties between British and Spanish officials and various Native American tribes made simple solutions unlikely. A collision with any one of these powers on or within the borders of the United States seemed certain to end in a war that included all three. Such local disputes seemed to present the greatest danger of dragging the United States into a new war—greater than the renewal of a general war in Europe or the launching of a deliberate attack from across the Atlantic. But Adams and Monroe also saw these disputes as the most susceptible to their control, making conflicts on the nation's borders the most preventable, as well as the most probable, source of an unwelcome war.[3]

Great Britain remained at the center of American fears when Adams took over the State Department. Two-and-a-half years after the War of 1812, relations remained tense. Its naval force, nearby colonies, and extensive trade provided Great Britain with various ways to injure the United States. And, in the fall of 1817, a wide range of disputes between the two powers awaited resolution. The boundary between the United States and British Canada from the Lake of the Woods to the Rocky Mountains remained undefined, even as British and American officials advanced conflicting claims to the Oregon country on the Pacific Coast. American fishing rights off Canada were another source of discussion, as were a handful of relatively minor issues that the Treaty of Ghent had only imperfectly addressed. The treaty had also left entirely unresolved all of the questions of neutral rights and impressment that had led to the war. Finally, the commercial Convention of 1815 had never really satisfied American desires for access to British colonial markets; it was, moreover, due to expire in 1819. Both British and American policymakers preferred peace—as shown, in part, by the recently signed Rush-Bagot Agreement. And most of the outstanding issues with Great Britain appeared amenable to a peaceful resolution. Accordingly, the most likely source of a rupture with Great Britain, in the thinking of Adams and Monroe, was a war with its Spanish ally or its Native American friends.

Officially, the secretary of state did not need to concern himself with Indian affairs; they were the province of Secretary of War John C. Calhoun. But Adams—along with Calhoun, Monroe, and most policymakers of the time—recognized that the presumably domestic relations with Native Americans could easily become entangled with the more obviously foreign relations with European powers, particularly Great Britain and Spain. This entanglement remained especially strong, in the fall of 1817, on the southern frontier. During the War of 1812, Red Stick Creeks from Alabama and Georgia had fought, first, other Creeks and, later, a mixed force of federal troops, state militiamen, and other tribes in an effort to check the onslaught of white culture and white settlers. After their defeat in the spring of 1814, the Red Sticks had fled to Spanish Florida, where they merged with the Seminoles. Even after the end of the Anglo-American war in the spring of 1815 and the destruction of an important Seminole fort in north Florida by American forces in the summer of 1816, the Seminoles continued to harass American surveyors and settlers in Georgia and Alabama. During the War of 1812, the Red Sticks and Seminoles had received support from the British Army. While this support had ended by the fall of 1817, they remained closely tied to British fur traders and appeared to have at least some support from Spanish officials in Pensacola and St. Augustine. It might be possible to isolate Native American problems from "foreign" affairs. But, as Adams recognized, it seemed more probable that trying to put down the Seminoles in Florida by force not only would lead to "a troublesome Indian war" but also could have an "extensive and important" impact "upon our political affairs."[4]

Throughout the postwar period, a rupture with Spain always seemed to pose the greatest threat of engulfing the United States in a new war. Territorial, commercial, and political questions divided the two nations. Spain, which had never fully accepted the legitimacy of the Louisiana Purchase, flatly rejected the American claim that Louisiana extended east to the Perdido River and west to the Rio Grande and strongly protested the American seizure of West Florida in 1810 and 1813. Following the War of 1812, American policymakers insisted as well upon acquiring East Florida, which had been used by the British and the Seminoles for attacks on the southern frontier. American merchants also looked to Spain for compensation for claims that dated back to the turn of the century. Spain, in turn, demanded that the federal government take greater pains to prevent American citizens from invading its North American colonies (as filibusters) and serving on the ships of its rebellious South American colonies (as privateers). These issues had formed the subject of a series of notably unsuccessful negotations between Spain and the United States in the fifteen years before Adams took over the State Department. Adams had no doubt that the British were carefully watching Spanish-American affairs. While in London, he had received an unmistakable, verbal warning from Viscount Castlereagh against "pursuing a system of encroachment upon your neighbors" that was clearly directed at Florida. Adams had also discerned "a perpetual tendency to interference" in favor of Spain against its rebellious colonies in all of the European powers "and in none more than [Great Britain]."[5]

Thus, most of the "hard knots" that Adams expected to have to untangle when he became secretary of state concerned the immediate neighborhood of the United States—Oregon, Florida, the northern and western borders, and the Canadian fisheries. Those that did not—particularly those generated by the Spanish American revolutions—still needed to be evaluated in terms of their potential to produce a war with the country's Spanish, Native American, and, especially, British neighbors. Important American interests were at stake in a number of areas in the fall of 1817, but Monroe and Adams continued to believe that prolonging the peace was more valuable to the United States at present than securing these interests. A concerted effort to acquire new territory in Texas, Florida, or Oregon or to open new markets in the British West Indies or Spanish South America, they worried, might lead to a war that would certainly carry great costs in American lives, wealth, and reputation and—Adams feared—could even destroy the union. A willingness to accept delays and postpone solutions to these critical issues seemed better-suited to long-term American interests than aggressive efforts on behalf of territorial and commercial expansion. Monroe and Adams were not willing to concede any important interests permanently, but were prepared to conciliate their neighbors temporarily. They expected to use the delays to their advantage, however, by strengthening the American position for any future negotiations. Adams, in particular, wanted to extend the federal government's power over the people, the executive branch's sway over its subordinate officials and Congress, and his own control over the State Department, the cabinet, and the president.[6]

Any effort to increase the federal government's power over the American people, Adams understood, would have to be handled very carefully. He had no intention of squelching the private energies that led American merchants to new markets and American settlers to new lands. Furthermore, Adams had long recognized that a republic simply could not exert the same kind of control over its citizens as a monarchy could over its subjects. Before taking over the State Department, he had often found ways to use the known weakness of republican governments to diplomatic advantage. In one of his first official notes as secretary of state, he deflected a complaint by reminding the French minister of the limits to "the repressive powers of the government." If the federal government was going to assert more control over its citizens, he believed, it would have to do so in a manner that would not encourage other nations to make new demands upon it. With thousands of Americans outfitting privateering vessels to seize merchant ships on behalf of the Spanish American revolutions and assembling filibustering expeditions to invade Spanish Texas and Florida, however, something had to be done. The Spanish, French, and Portuguese ministers barraged Adams with complaints. It quickly became clear that the illegal acts of American privateers and filibusters not only "degrade[d] the Nation in the Eyes of the World" but also "essentially endanger[ed] its Peace." For Adams to maintain peace in the short-term and enhance his bargaining position in the long-term, the federal government had to find some way to suppress these activities.[7]

Adams considered it no less important, and presumably much easier, to increase the executive branch's control over its own subordinates. He quickly discovered, as Monroe had before him, that the administration's representatives in the field often undermined its efforts and threatened the peace by pursuing their own interpretation of American interests on their own authority. In Europe and, especially, Spanish America, American diplomats—ministers, consuls, and agents—took it upon themselves to make commitments and even sign treaties without instructions. At home, customs collectors, district attornies, and navy officers ignored, and at times aided, the outfitting of privateers in ports on the Atlantic and Gulf coasts, while army officers and territorial officials permitted, and even launched, incursions into Spanish and Indian lands on the

southern frontier. Although Adams formally disputed the asper-
sion, he privately recognized the justice of the Portuguese minister's
characterization of the federal officials in Baltimore—a notorious
privateering center—as "'a most unmanageable crew.'" "The officers of the United States," Adams admitted in his diary, "have been
the principal causes, by connivance, or by something worse, of all
the piracies which for these three or four years have issued from
that city." Bringing under closer control subordinates overseas, in
ports, and on the frontiers seemed essential to preserving the peace.
It also appeared critical to Adams's future negotiations. It would
be impossible for him to manipulate the carrots and sticks of diplomacy unless he could count on the government's agents in the
field to act as he expected and directed.[8]

In Adams's thinking, preventing interference by the other
branches of the federal government, particularly Congress, seemed
no less necessary for augmenting the executive branch's ability to
determine and implement foreign policy. Adams viewed foreign
affairs in general as "strictly an Executive act" and considered it an
"absurdity" that "Congress, instead of the Executive," held "the
power of declaring war." This "error" had unfortunately provided
Congress with the grounds for entering into foreign policy issues
whenever they "involv[ed] the question of peace and war." Over
the preceding three decades, one result had been the public exposure of most of the inner workings of American policymaking to
everyone, friend or foe. Another had been occasional efforts by
congressional leaders to use foreign policy issues "to control or
overthrow the Executive." Adams knew that he could not change
the Constitution, but he could certainly assert the prerogatives of
the executive branch on foreign policy issues in any disputed case.
In fact, he hoped to do much more. As secretary of state, he repeatedly attempted to make Congress serve the will of the executive on
such issues. He did not intend for Congress to ignore foreign relations entirely. Instead, he wanted it to act when and as the executive directed, debating foreign policy issues, calling for diplomatic
correspondence, passing neutrality legislation, and even authorizing aggressive actions—but only when those steps would bolster
his negotiations.[9]

When Adams entered office in the fall of 1817, he believed that
it would be necessary to strengthen not only the federal government's position in the political system and the executive branch's
position in the federal government but also his own position in the
executive branch. One of the easiest ways to accomplish this goal,

he thought, would be to systematize the operations of the State Department itself. On his first day at the office, Adams found the business of the department "much in arrear." He quickly attempted to overcome this "great confusion" by establishing "a proper system of order" that included having daily records made of all incoming correspondence and drafting a set of standard instructions for each rank of American diplomats abroad. He envisioned even more ambitious steps, such as making indexes that abstracted the contents and listed the enclosures of "each dispatch from every Minister abroad," from every consul, and from each of "the foreign Ministers here." Greater order in the department office, Adams could reasonably hope, would result in more faithful service from diplomats in the field, who could turn to clear instructions and prompt replies to their questions to guide their actions. But he also calculated that, the more smoothly the State Department worked, the more forcefully and effectively he would be able to assert his policy suggestions in executive deliberations.[10]

From the beginning, Adams had understood that his ability to achieve his goals as secretary of state would depend, to a great degree, upon his success at influencing the other cabinet members and the president. It was "the nature of the thing," he informed his mother four months before taking over the department, that a cabinet would be composed of men who were "equal in trust, justly confident of their abilities, disdainful of influence, yet eager to exercise it, impatient of control, and . . . resistan[t] to surmises and phantoms of encroachment" by their colleagues. As soon as the cabinet began to meet regularly, Adams assessed "the characters of [his] colleagues." He admired Calhoun's "sound judgment" and independent mind, determined that Attorney General William Wirt and Secretary of the Navy Benjamin Crowninshield would "always be of the President's opinion," and concluded that Secretary of the Treasury William H. Crawford considered it a point of honor "to differ from me, and to find no weight in any reason assigned by me." Adams also recognized early on that the president would give equal consideration to the views of each of his cabinet members and preferred to act only after a consensus had been reached. This insistence upon consensus led Adams, over the course of Monroe's presidency, into various forms of trickery to ensure that his positions triumphed. At one point, he decided that he should never speak on behalf of his positions if Monroe already favored them in order to avoid provoking Crawford into speaking against them. In time, moreover, Adams resorted to the subterfuge of inserting passages that he wanted eliminated into the drafts of his dispatches before the cabinet considered them in order "to absorb that portion of the objecting spirit which must find exercise upon something."[11]

In retrospect, some of Adams's clashes with other cabinet members and some of his machinations in support of his policies seem petty. But, at least in his mind, they were merely another aspect of his efforts to preserve an uncertain peace and enhance his, and his successors', bargaining position with other powers. He foresaw, as the eventual reward for these efforts, success in negotiations that would help to produce a more secure and more durable union. As a New Englander, he understood the necessity of protecting and promoting maritime and commercial interests—such as access to the Canadian fisheries and colonial markets—for securing the loyalty of one important section of the union. But, as important as a global vision of American commercial expansion was for Adams, he placed even greater emphasis upon his continental vision of American territorial expansion. For Adams, the entirety of North America, including the remaining Spanish and British colonies, had to be viewed as "our natural dominion." In time, the American people would spread across the continent, transforming "howling deserts into cultivated fields and populous villages." Nothing, Adams believed, could thwart that process. This movement of the people would not necessarily lead to the expansion of the American nation. Yet Adams considered it "indispensable" to the "common happiness" of all Americans "that they should be associated in one federal Union"; otherwise, "America like the rest of the earth [would] sink into a common field of battle for conquerors and tyrants." If commercial and, especially, territorial expansion was to perpetuate, rather than destroy, the union and promote, rather than undermine, the ends that the union was meant to secure, it would require the kind of sophisticated diplomacy that was widely believed to be impossible for a republic; Adams's efforts were intended to make it possible.[12]

Adams undertook the duties of the secretary of state, and entered into a position that he considered more "critical and precarious" than any that he had previously accepted, with some very clear ideas. He considered the union's crucial interests to be continued peace in the short-term and carefully managed commercial and territorial expansion in the long-term. He believed that both sets of interests, short- and long-term, would be better served by postponing the resolution of most of the issues disputed by the

United States and its Spanish and British neighbors. And he intended to make good use of the resulting delays with a multifaceted effort to strengthen the American position in the eventual negotiations. Despite Adams's persistent fears that "the path before [him was] beset with thorns," there appeared to be good reason to expect success in each of his short-, medium-, and long-term goals.[13]

~

Adams's first eighteen months in office produced a pair of significant accomplishments—the Convention of 1818 with Great Britain and the Transcontinental Treaty with Spain. These two agreements resolved a wide range of outstanding disputes with the country's most important neighbors. But these dramatic changes came about in ways entirely unforeseen by Monroe and Adams. They required neither the willingness to accept delays nor the ability to control all aspects of American foreign relations that Adams, in particular, believed necessary. In other words, developments that were expected only in the long-term—territorial and commercial expansion—instead happened in the short-term. And they happened without either sparking a war for which the United States was unprepared or awaiting the outcome of Adams's efforts to improve his bargaining position. The great irony of Adams's diplomatic successes, in fact, was that they derived from the temporary abandonment or outright failure of his efforts to extend his control over policymaking. A recognition of this irony should not lessen Adams's achievement. These agreements did not come about in the way that he expected, but they did require skillful diplomacy on his part. Unable to control events as he had intended, he showed tremendous creativity in using unexpected and undesired events to his, and his country's, advantage.

On the very day that he arrived in Washington to take over the State Department, Adams "convers[ed] upon the state of the public relations with Great Britain, Spain, and France" with the president; over the next few weeks, he began direct discussions with the British, Spanish, and French ministers—Charles Bagot, Don Luis de Onís, and Baron Guillaume Hyde de Neuville. Monroe and Adams considered these negotiations important, but they did not expect them to resolve the most significant disputes with these powers. A new or renewed commercial convention with Great Britain certainly seemed likely, as did an agreement to have at least some of the problems arising from the Treaty of Ghent decided by an outside arbitrator. And early resolutions of the fisheries question and the Canadian-American boundary east of the Rockies appeared possible. The same could hardly have been said of the Canadian-American boundary west of the Rockies—the Oregon question—or of any of the issues in dispute with Spain—Florida, the Mexican-American boundary, or the damage claims. But negotiations could serve the immediate goal of preserving the peace even if there was little prospect of them achieving their long-term goals. Adams would negotiate with Onís, and would make sure that Bagot and Hyde de Neuville knew of his efforts, because negotiations would help to prevent a rupture or, at least, to limit its scope if one occurred. But, viewing delay as an ally of the United States, he would not press for a hasty treaty. Writing to Onís after three months of inconclusive negotiations, Adams accurately, if sarcastically, captured the administration's thinking when he explained that the United States, having waited thirteen years for "a happy and harmonious termination" of the dispute, would "need little additional effort to wait somewhat longer with the same expectation."[14]

The United States would wait, but it would not wait idly. Some of the benefits that Monroe and Adams expected to come from further delays were almost entirely outside their control. They certainly anticipated a gradual erosion of Spain's European, and especially British, support resulting from future developments in Europe that would demand the attention of the Great Powers. And they looked to a further weakening of Spain's position driven by the success of the revolutionary movements in its South American colonies. They also imagined an active role for themselves. They continued the multifaceted postwar efforts on behalf of military preparedness and worked to isolate Spain from its potential British and Native American allies. Adams, especially, sought to bring all of the elements of American foreign relations under the control of the executive branch, in general, and himself, in particular. He had hardly even begun this process, however, when a series of developments that he could not control, and did not welcome, prompted Spain to make the sweeping concessions that were necessary for a treaty. Congressional "interference" in foreign policy and unsanctioned actions by a subordinate officer in the field broke open the deadlocked negotiations. At the same time, they forced Adams into some very creative policymaking and very skillful maneuvering in order to prevent a war and turn these developments to his advantage.

In his first months in office, Adams faced what he saw as a challenge to executive branch control over foreign policy in the form of congressional discussion of American neutrality in the conflict between Spain and its rebellious colonies. Unlike many of his countrymen, Adams viewed with great skepticism the idea that "the cause of the South Americans [was] . . . the same as our own cause in the war of our Revolution." He also believed that, if the United States tilted too obviously toward the colonists, especially by extending formal diplomatic recognition of their independence, it would find itself embroiled in a war not only with Spain but also with Great Britain. Neutrality, in general, and recognition, in particular, however, emerged as key issues during the congressional session that lasted from December 1817 to April 1818. Even before the session began, Speaker of the House Henry Clay had worked through various channels to press the president to take a bold stand in favor of the revolutions in his annual message to Congress. When Monroe, at Adams's urging, demurred, Clay immediately brought the neutrality issue before the House himself. Over the course of the session, the House debated a revision of the neutrality laws, an administration decision to break up a privateering base at Amelia Island (on the Georgia-Florida border), and a motion by Clay to set aside funds for a minister to Buenos Aires. A distressed Adams certainly overstated the force of this motion when he viewed it as "merely a mode of proposing a formal [recognition]." Still, if it had passed, it clearly would have indicated congressional support for recognition and increased the pressure on Monroe to take a step that Adams considered dangerous.[15]

An even greater threat to Adams's commitment to preserving the peace emerged during the spring of 1818 when, just as he had feared, the war against the Seminoles spilled over into Spanish forts in northern Florida. When Monroe and Calhoun transferred responsibility for this war to General Andrew Jackson in late December 1817, they clearly expected him to adhere to the very cautious instructions that had been sent to his predecessor. As Jackson made his preparations in late January, Monroe further directed Calhoun to "instruct him not to attack any post occupied by Spanish troops, from the possibility, that it might bring the allied powers on us." But Jackson had a long history of acting on his own discretion when he thought that his superiors did not fully understand the situation that he faced. He started the campaign concerned that obedience to the limits set down by Monroe and Calhoun could end in "catastrophe" and convinced that "the whole of East Florida [should be] seized and held." And he could find just enough ambiguity in his correspondence with the administration to justify, in his own mind, whatever steps he decided to take. With a force of nearly five thousand federal regulars, Tennessee militiamen, and Creeks, Jackson launched his invasion of Florida in March. Over the next ten weeks, his men destroyed a number of Seminole villages, built a garrison on the Apalachicola River in Spanish territory, and captured the Spanish forts at St. Marks and Pensacola. Jackson also had executed two British subjects, Alexander Arbuthnot and Robert Ambrister, who were found among the Seminoles. Finally, in orders that were quickly countermanded by Calhoun, he ordered a subordinate to capture St. Augustine.[16]

Ultimately, the combined effect of the push for recognition and the invasion of Florida convinced the Spanish king and his cabinet that they could not afford to stall any longer. They had long been willing to cede Florida, but had wanted to receive in exchange a favorable border between Mexico and the United States (one as close to the Mississippi River as possible) and American agreements to assume the damage claims of its merchants, to enact stricter neutrality laws, and to foreswear recognition of any of Spain's colonies. The developments in Congress and in Florida suggested that, unless Spain made a deal quickly, it would lose Florida before it could trade it and would find its colonies recognized by the United States. A year earlier, neither Spanish nor American policymakers would have predicted this result. While Onís and Adams agreed on few points in the early months of their negotiations, they could have easily agreed that the outcome of either the recognition of the Spanish colonies or the seizure of Florida would have certainly been a rupture, possibly a war, but definitely not a treaty. Once the negotiations had ended and the Transcontinental Treaty had been signed, however, Adams noted the critical role of Clay's and Jackson's actions. Congressional pressure for recognition, he admitted in his diary, "contributed to promot[ing] the conclusion of the treaty." Jackson's rampage through Florida seemed even more significant. "The transactions of his campaign," in Adams's assessment, were "among the most immediate and prominent causes that produced [the] treaty."[17]

If Adams had carefully masterminded Clay's and Jackson's actions, thus orchestrating the pressures that led to the Spanish government to accept a treaty on American terms, he would have established a strong claim to being precisely the kind of master diplomat that many historians have portrayed. In fact, Adams had not orchestrated them at all. He had opposed Clay's support for recognition from the moment that he learned of it, just days after taking over the State Department. Throughout the congressional session, he did everything he could to thwart what he saw as an assault on the power of the executive branch and a threat to the peace of the United States. And he had positively thrilled at the failure of Clay's motion to set aside funds for a minister to Buenos Aires, describing it as just another part of the "tragi-Comedy of passion for South America." Adams also bore no responsibility for Jackson's seizure of the Spanish forts. The general had been ordered into Florida by Monroe and Calhoun "without my being consulted, and without my knowledge." "There was no other member of the Administration," he informed his father, "who had less or even so little concern with [Jackson's actions], or agency over them, until long after they were past and irretrievable." It was precisely when these developments were "past and irretrievable," however, that Adams's brilliance became clear. He managed to play the cards that he had been dealt—cards that he very clearly had not wanted—in ways that forced the Spanish cabinet to recognize the weakness of its own hand.[18]

Clay's intention, as Adams understood it, had been "to push the Executive, if possible, into a quarrel with Spain" as a means of bringing the United States into the Spanish colonial conflict on the side of the revolutionaries. But Clay had "not play[ed] his game very skilfully." He had "alarmed Spain," but "without involving the Executive." As such, Adams discovered that Clay had put him in a position where he could juxtapose the cabinet's reserve to Congress's "impetuosity." In meetings with Onís and, especially, Hyde de Neuville in December 1818 and January 1819, Adams hinted that Spain might "postpon[e] further a recognition" by signing a treaty. Adams would not make any "guarantee, verbal or written, express or implied." But he did explain to Hyde de Neuville what might already have happened "if Spain had taken the pains to adjust her differences with us[—]there would probably be much less ardor in this country against Spain, and consequently less in favor of the South Americans." Without saying so directly, Adams clearly intended for Hyde de Neuville, and through him Onís, to assume that the same process would play out in the future if Spain quickly signed an acceptable treaty. Popular enthusiasm for the revolutions and hostility to Spain would wane; even fewer congressmen would support a measure that no longer captured the public's attention; the administration would regain control over foreign policy. Most important for Spain, Monroe and Adams could be expected to continue to act with restraint on the recognition question. In Adams's capable hands, Clay's pressure for recognition thus provided an "argument to bring [Spain] to reasonable terms."[19]

Adams needed even greater skill to turn Jackson's seizure of St. Marks and Pensacola to his advantage. As news of Jackson's rampage through Florida trickled into Washington in May and June 1818, Adams recognized that "the moment [was] very critical, and a storm [was] rapidly thickening." Notes from and meetings with the British, French, and Spanish ministers made evident their alarm. A war with the Spanish seemed likely and the involvement of the British, who were understandably upset by the executions of Ambrister (a Royal Marine) and Arbuthnot (a trader), appeared possible. The administration faced "a dilemma." If it "avow[ed] and approve[d] Jackson's conduct," Adams noted, it would "incur the double responsibility of having commenced a war against Spain, and of warring in violation of the Constitution." If it disavowed Jackson, it would "give offence to all his friends" and reinforce Spain's obstinacy in the negotiations. Monroe and the rest of the cabinet wanted to disavow Jackson for "act[ing] not only without, but against, his instructions." Instead, Adams found a middle course of offering to restore the Spanish forts while also justifying Jackson's seizures of them as measures of self-defense. By avoiding any "appearance of truckling to Spain," he convinced Onís that the United States would risk a war—a war that Spain could not afford—rather than abandon its territorial goals. When Adams also offered to concede American claims to Texas by drawing the western boundary at the Sabine River, Onís saw an opportunity to end the crisis by concluding a treaty that was more acceptable to Spain than any previously proposed.[20]

The combination of the carrot of territorial concessions and the stick of military threats may have impressed upon Onís the need for a quick treaty in the summer of 1818, but he lacked the necessary instructions to agree to a boundary line that began at the Sabine and extended, as Adams for the first time suggested, to the Pacific. As long as the Spanish cabinet believed that it could count on European, and particularly British, support in its dealings with the United States, such instructions were not going to be forthcoming. During the summer and early fall of 1818, two developments—only one of which Adams helped to produce—exposed the bankruptcy of this belief. The first—the one in which Adams had a part—was an emerging rapprochement between Great Britain and the United States. The clearest indication of this easing of Anglo-American tensions was the harmonious and successful nature of the negotiations in London that resulted in the Convention of 1818. Adams's instructions to Richard Rush and Albert Gallatin had fostered such harmony by directing them to avoid raising some controversial issues, such as neutral rights and impressment, and to accept temporary solutions for others, such as access to British colonial markets. More crucial in undermining Spain's position was Great Britain's successful effort to keep the Great Powers from assisting it in restoring control over its rebellious colonies. Even before the Great Powers convened at Aix-la-Chapelle in late September, the British had persuaded them not to invite the Spanish king and not to discuss armed intervention. Within weeks, the Spanish cabinet sent Onís carte blanche instructions and directed him to conclude a treaty on the best terms that he could convince Adams to accept.

Adams did not immediately grasp how thoroughly his support for Jackson, his willingness to make a concession on the western boundary, and Europe's failure to assist Spain against its rebel colonies had transformed the circumstances that had produced so many years of failed talks. In the months between the resumption of the negotiations in July 1818 and their conclusion in February 1819, he repeatedly sought ways to deal himself the stronger hand that he still believed would prove necessary to bring the talks to a successful close. His discussions of recognition with Hyde de Neuville in late December and early January certainly should be viewed in this way. In November and December, moreover, he wrote two bombastic letters to the American minister in Spain defending more stridently than ever before the administration's decision to send Jackson into Florida and Jackson's seizure of the Spanish forts. He claimed that these letters were "strictly and exclusively an answer to Spain and her complaints," but the speed with which he made them available to Congress and, thus, the public suggests that they were also intended to win support for stronger measures. Adams became increasingly convinced that such measures were needed the longer his negotiations with Onís, who did not receive his carte blanche instructions until late January, continued. From the start of the new congressional session in November, Adams suggested to the president and hinted to congressmen the importance of a grant of "authori[ty] to take Florida upon certain contingencies." By early January, he flatly concluded that the "prospect . . . of obtaining Florida by an arrangement with Spain" was "hopeless" without this authorization from Congress. "That might bring Spain to [a treaty]," but—he incorrectly advised Monroe—"nothing else would." In fact, a few more weeks of bargaining between Adams and Onís produced a treaty that had long appeared unobtainable.[21]

Adams could point to two significant diplomatic achievements by the end of his first eighteen months in office, the convention with Great Britain and the treaty with Spain. The Convention of 1818 resolved some outstanding issues and postponed others. It settled the Canadian fisheries dispute, fixed the border from the Lake of the Woods to the Rockies, assigned one of the remaining issues from the Treaty of Ghent to an outside arbitrator, and renewed the trading terms set by the Convention of 1815. At the same time, it said nothing about impressment, neutral rights, or American access to British colonial markets. And it explicitly postponed any definition of the boundary west of the Rockies and, thus, the disposition of the Oregon country by stating that the entire region would be open to settlement by American citizens and British subjects for ten years. It was on this potentially critical question that Adams's willingness to abandon his goal of bringing foreign relations more fully under the control of the federal government, the executive branch, and himself became most apparent. Adams preferred that the Oregon question not even be "include[d] among the objects of serious discussion" and provided Rush and Gallatin with no proposals on that point. By not even trying to fix a boundary in a region where "the present interest" of either the United States or Great Britain was small, Adams may have hoped to smooth the process of negotiations. But he also clearly believed that, with no government interference on either side, Americans were far more likely to settle Oregon than Canadians were. The federal government would better support American expansion in this area by keeping quiet—allowing the people gradually to settle the continent, while avoiding a formal arrangement with Great Britain "until all possibility of her preventing [this expansion] shall have vanished." While the convention ultimately did address the Oregon question, it did so in a manner consistent with Adams's plan to limit any government involvement and postpone a final resolution.[22]

Adams viewed the Transcontinental Treaty with Spain as far more important than the Convention of 1818. "Its prospects," he believed, were "propitious and flattering in an eminent degree"; the day of its ratification by the Senate "was, perhaps, the most important day of [his] life." In general terms, the treaty could be expected to transform Spanish-American relations "from the highest mutual exasperation and imminent war to a fair prospect of tranquillity and of secure peace." In more specific terms, the United States acquired Florida, long "an object of earnest desire to this country." It strengthened its claim to the Oregon country through Spain's agreement to a boundary between Mexico and the United States that extended along the 42nd parallel to the Pacific. In exchange, the United States assumed the damage claims of American citizens against Spain up to a total of five million dollars. And it surrendered its weak claims to Texas by accepting a boundary on the Gulf of Mexico at the Sabine. Even at the pinnacle of his excitement about and pride in the treaty, however, Adams recognized that it had not come about in the way that he had expected or planned. In his diary, he attributed it to "the all-wise and all-beneficent Disposer of events, who [had] brought it about in a manner utterly unexpected and by means the most extraordinary and unforeseen." Ten months earlier, he had commented that "there never had been a negotiation . . . upon which there was so little prospect that the parties would ever come to an understanding." It required "extraordinary and unforeseen" developments in Congress, in Florida, and in Europe to produce so quickly a treaty that Adams had expected would take years of hard work.[23]

At the end of April 1819, Adams assessed the previous six or seven months. This brief interval had "probably been in relation to public affairs among the most important, and incomparably the most successful period of my life, past or future." Adams had accomplished his short-term goal of preserving what he considered an essential and precarious peace with Spain and Great Britain. And he had unexpectedly achieved, at least in part, his long-term goals of territorial and commercial expansion by acquiring Florida and improving American claims on the Pacific—thus facilitating American participation in both the fur trade and the China trade. Despite the abandonment of American claims to Texas, moreover, Adams could still insist that the treaty with Spain "rendered it still more unavoidable that the remainder of the continent should ultimately be ours." Still, he had made very little progress in his medium-term goal of extending his control over American foreign relations. As a result, the Convention of 1818 and the Transcontinental Treaty had derived more from unexpected developments—and from Adams's skill at making good use of them—than from careful policymaking. It soon became apparent that they would foster new conflicts at home and abroad rather than produce the more stable union and more secure peace that Adams had predicted.[24]

~

Between February 1819 and February 1821, the United States was engulfed in a multifaceted crisis that intensified sectional tensions and undermined federal power and authority. A severe economic downturn—the Panic of 1819—and a heated congressional debate over the expansion of slavery beyond the Mississippi—the Missouri Crisis—formed the two central elements of a crisis that "alarm[ed Adams] greatly for the continuance of this Union." The successes and the failures of Adams's first months in office, moreover, helped to fuel the crisis by complicating the sectional divisions and adding an international dimension. Because Adams had failed, and continued to fail, to gain control over the full range of American foreign relations in the way that he intended, the Transcontinental Treaty and, to a much smaller degree, the Convention of 1818 emerged as problems rather than solutions, generating internal debate and external tension. Failure at the medium-term goal of asserting control over foreign relations, in effect, threatened the short-term goal of continued peace, the long-term goal of territorial and commercial expansion, and the ultimate goal of a stronger union in the two years after the signing of the Transcontinental Treaty.[25]

The result of changes in the European economy and weaknesses in the American banking system, the Panic of 1819 spread economic hardship throughout the United States. Businesses failed; banks closed; artisans and factory workers lost their jobs; farmers and planters faced falling prices. Its effects were not limited to financial and economic issues. The Panic of 1819 also had a dramatic impact upon domestic politics. For one thing, it increased sectional tensions. The agricultural districts of the South and West suffered much more from the Panic than the commercial centers of the Northeast. As they saw their scarce specie flowing steadily to Boston, New York, Philadelphia, and Washington to pay for imported goods and land, southerners and westerners began to clamor for political solutions. Adams predicted early in the Panic that "even the tranquillity of the Union [would] be most seriously affected by it." Furthermore, "as always happens, the disorder of things [produced] discord of opinions and bitterness of political opposition." The

Panic heightened and transformed party divisions, especially within the states. Finally, it seriously undermined federal power and authority. Plummeting land sales and customs receipts cut into annual revenues, leaving the government without enough money to undertake any new projects and threatening the funding for the expanded army and navy and the new fortifications that had formed the core of postwar military preparedness. At the same time, many Americans showed little respect for a government that they saw as simultaneously responsible for their woes—particularly through the Bank of the United States and the Land Office—and unwilling to ease them.[26]

The crisis over the admission of Missouri as a slave state, which began in January 1819 and ended only in February 1821, had the same corrosive effects on the stability of the union and the energy of the federal government as the Panic of 1819. Northern congressmen wanted Missouri to be admitted to the union only if the further importation of slaves was prohibited and the eventual emancipation of those already in the state was assured. Southern congressmen opposed any restrictions on Missouri's admission as a slave state. The obvious North-South division over the slavery question masked western concerns that all of the future states formed from the Louisiana Purchase would have to accept limits on their sovereignty that did not apply to the eastern states. The union faced its greatest challenge since the War of 1812. In Congress and throughout Washington, Clay reported, "the words, civil war, and disunion, are uttered almost without emotion." In March 1820, Clay helped to put together a compromise under which Missouri was admitted as a slave state, Maine (formerly a part of Massachusetts) was admitted as a free state, and a line was drawn across the rest of the Louisiana Purchase at 36°30' to separate slave and free territories. A year later, he engineered a second compromise after Congress divided once again over the language of Missouri's constitution. Still, for three successive sessions, the Missouri Crisis, as Clay lamented, "disqualified Congress for all sorts of other business" by "absorb[ing] all attention." Federal energy suffered as "every other matter of public concern" awaited the outcome of the divisive Missouri debates.[27]

Adams's recent successes, particularly the Transcontinental Treaty, intensified this crisis in two ways. For one thing, the terms of the treaty deepened the concerns raised by the Missouri Crisis in every section. Some northerners worried about the expansion of slavery into the newly acquired territories to the south and west. "The Missouri question and its compromise," Adams recorded in March 1820, "[gave] the Northern and Eastern interest a distaste even for Florida, because that would become another slave State." Conversely, the Missouri Crisis tended "[to sharpen] the greediness of the Southern interest for more Southern Territories to make more slave States." In combination, however, the Missouri Compromise line and the Transcontinental Treaty line reserved only a relatively small part of the region beyond the Mississippi for new slave states. Southerners quickly began to complain about the abandonment of the American claim to Texas—an immense territory that seemed well suited to slavery and lay south of the 36°30′ line. Their complaints echoed those of some westerners, who had criticized the treaty from the very start for surrendering American claims to the region between the Sabine and the Rio Grande. The abandonment of Texas seemed to these westerners a further example of the federal government's willingness to sacrifice western interests, joining Congress's effort to restrict Missouri statehood, the Bank of the United States's and the Land Office's mishandling of the Panic of 1819, and a number of other domestic and foreign policies in their catalogue of injustices.[28]

To make matters worse, the Transcontinental Treaty itself was in a state of great uncertainty for much of the period of the Missouri debates, providing an international dimension to the crisis. The Senate ratified the treaty unanimously in February 1819, and Onís returned with it to Spain. But the king refused to ratify within the allotted six months. The nonratification of the treaty left Monroe and Adams with a bewildering array of policy choices from immediately seizing Florida and perhaps Texas to resuming negotiations with a new Spanish minister who did not even reach the United States until April 1820. Initially, the cabinet leaned toward occupying Florida by force and treating the treaty as if it had been ratified. Adams alerted his ministers in Europe to expect such a course; Calhoun requested information from Jackson on the disposition of Spanish forces in Florida; and Monroe sought congressional authorization in his annual message of December 1819. Monroe and Adams expected that Florida could be taken "without any views of hostility to Spain" and without "disturb[ing] the Peace of Europe." The reaction of the various European ministers in Washington suggested otherwise. As the crisis over the treaty unfolded, Monroe and Adams became increasingly convinced that Great Britain,

France, and Russia "had a strong interest of their own" in the controversy—"the interest of general peace, which was threatened with imminent danger, in the event of a war between us and Spain." As had been the case for much of the postwar era, a patient and conciliatory approach to the dispute with Spain once again seemed essential to preserving the peace and acquiring new territory.[29]

Ironically, the treaty's nonratification derived from the same failure of Adams's efforts to take control over American foreign relations as its initial signing. Adams had always known that extending the authority of the federal government over the people would be a long and difficult process. He had quickly discovered that asserting the predominance of the executive over the legislature in foreign affairs would be resisted by key congressmen, especially Clay. More surprising, however, is that Adams proved incapable of increasing his control even within the State Department and the cabinet where his chances had seemed most promising. His attempts to bring order to the daily operations of the department barely addressed the problems. In May 1819, he foresaw that, of the many projects for reforming the department that "arise and flit across my mind like the shadows of a phantasmogoria[,] . . . not one of them will ever be executed." He expected to "leave the Office as [he] found it—a Chaos of Confusion." Adams made no more headway with the goal of holding in line distant subordinates, in part because Monroe kept the choice of officeholders "very much in his own hands." With none of the appointments "made at [his] recommendation" or even with his approval, Adams could only recall these officials after they misbehaved. Finally, Adams never gained the influence within the cabinet that he had wanted. He attributed this failure partly to Crawford, whom he viewed as "a worm preying upon the vitals of the Administration within its own body," and partly to Monroe, who hesitated to adopt policies without reaching a consensus. But Adams also seems to have understood that his personality—he described himself as "a man of reserved, cold, austere, and forbidding manners"—may have contributed to his problems in the cabinet.[30]

The more that Adams learned about Spain's refusal to ratify the Transcontinental Treaty, the more completely he blamed forces and individuals that he could not control. Initially, he traced the nonratification of the treaty to a mistake of his own regarding the date of land grants in Florida to a group of Spanish nobles. In late November 1819, however, Hyde de Neuville explained that "it was not the affair of the grants" at all. Instead, the Spanish king feared "that if he should ratify the treaty, the next day [the United States] should recognize the South Americans and make a common cause with them." Adams could point to a number of developments that might have fed this fear, all of which were, in his view, traceable to Monroe rather than himself. It had been the president who, ignoring Adams's counsel, had proposed to the British a joint Anglo-American recognition of one or more of the Spanish American governments in the summer and fall of 1818. It had been Monroe who, again defying Adams's advice, had appointed a notorious supporter of privateering as federal judge in Baltimore. And it had been the president who had "omi[tted] to issue a proclamation" against a filibustering expedition into Texas in the summer of 1819 and who had included remarks in favor of "South American independence in [his] messages to Congress." "None of these measures have been mine," Adams recorded in his diary, "nor have they been congenial to the rest of the system." While Adams described these measures as "imputable entirely to the President," they provide evidence as well of his failure to extend the federal government's control over the people—in the case of the filibustering expedition—and the executive branch's sway over its subordinates—in the case of the Baltimore judge.[31]

Adams's inability to prevent congressional interference in foreign relations posed additional challenges. For one thing, the failure of the Transcontinental Treaty led Clay to renew his efforts to influence administration policies. Opposed to the treaty for unnecessarily ceding Texas and convinced that Spain would not risk war, Clay called for the occupation of Texas as a part of the United States and the recognition of Spanish American independence. In May 1820 and again in February 1821, he pushed mildly worded resolutions in support of recognition through the House that brought concerned French and Spanish ministers rushing to Adams's office. More important, in January 1821 a committee chaired by John Floyd submitted a report to the House that sparked a brief, but intense, collision over Oregon between Adams and the new British minister, Stratford Canning. Floyd and his mostly western supporters were dissatisfied with both the Transcontinental Treaty's abandonment of Texas and the Convention of 1818's postponement of the Oregon question. He publicly argued that no nations other than the United States and Spain had claims to the Pacific coast south of 60° north latitude, denying British and Russian claims. The Floyd report also called for a federally supported settlement along the Columbia River as a way to bolster American participation in the fur and China trades. Engrossed in the Missouri debates, Congress never took up these proposals. But Canning called upon Adams for an explanation, leading to a series of fiery meetings that seriously damaged the personal relations between the two men, though not the official relations between their governments.

Adams approached Spain's refusal to ratify the treaty in the same way that he had approached its earlier refusal to accept the concessions necessary to conclude one. He attempted both to manipulate the developments that he could not control to his own purposes and to orchestrate the incentives and pressures that he believed would lead the Spanish king to ratify. The success of Clay's May 1820 resolution in favor of recognition, for example, gave Adams, once again, a way to highlight the administration's reserve on this issue. "The President," Adams informed Hyde de Neuville on the day after the vote, "intended no change of policy with regard to South America for the present." Aware that the president's past messages to Congress had undermined this claim to caution, moreover, Adams worked diligently to increase his influence over Monroe. As soon as he understood the link between recognition and ratification, Adams began pressuring Monroe to revise his almost complete annual message, arguing that the administration "should avoid anything of which Spain might make a handle, and which would dispose France and Russia against us." Adams also urged a stronger stand, both in the message and in reality, against privateering and filibustering, which led to improved enforcement in subsequent months. Ultimately, however, it took unexpected developments in Europe to finalize the treaty, just as it had to complete it. In the midst of a crisis that included economic, political, sectional, and diplomatic aspects, the administration could never devise and implement the kind of energetic policies that might have put pressure on Spain. Instead, a revolution in Spain in the spring of 1820 brought to power a constitutional government that was willing to ratify the treaty, allowing it to take effect in early 1821.[32]

Between the Senate's ratification of the Transcontinental Treaty in February 1819 and its reratification two years later, the United States faced a multifaceted crisis that showed the validity of Adams's longstanding concerns, the significance of his ongoing failures, and the hollowness of his recent successes. For Adams, as for many other policymakers, this serious crisis provided startling evidence of the continuing fragility of the union and the lingering infirmity of the federal government. The Founders' old fears that the union could dissolve and that its dissolution could lead to conflict and war among American states that would destroy the Revolution gained renewed force. The achievement of long-term territorial and commercial goals through the recently signed agreements with Spain and Great Britain had done nothing to ease this crisis. In fact, the exchange of Texas for a boundary to the Pacific, the acquisition of Florida, and the recognition of British interest in Oregon had intensified the divisions between the sections and the frictions between the administration and Congress. In the midst of the crisis, Adams began to question, if not the goal of continentalism, at least the pace of American expansion. "The greatest danger of this Union," he reflected in April 1820, "was in the overgrown extent of its territory, combining with the slavery question." Even with the Transcontinental Treaty, he worried that the United States would acquire Texas "sooner than we should want it" since its acquisition might "ultimately break us up." Adams ended his first term as secretary of state as convinced as ever of the importance of shaping policy with an eye on the stability of the union.[33]

~

With the Missouri Crisis once again compromised, the Panic of 1819 at least easing, and the Transcontinental Treaty finally completed in late February 1821, Adams could offer a generally positive assessment of the preceding four years. "The conduct of the Administration [had] been, upon the whole, wise, honest, and patriotic," though there was no question that it had also "been blessed with good fortune." He could "look back with satisfaction solid and pure at what [had] been accomplished of public service" by his own efforts, though not without "humility and regret that more [had] not been effected." In a sense, his first term as secretary of state had centered on precisely the problem that he had foreseen would be central when he accepted the position—the difficulty of prolonging a peace that seemed critical to the union in the face of tensions in its immediate neighborhood. Adams had, in fact, helped to preserve the peace and ease the tensions with Spain and Great Britain. But he had intended to accomplish these short-term goals, and to strengthen future efforts to achieve the long-term goals of territorial and commercial expansion, more through his own control over American foreign relations than through the unreliable assistance of "the Disposer of all results." It had never occurred to him, moreover, that the unexpected fulfillment of some of his long-term goals might undermine the very ends to which they were directed—a more durable union and a more energetic government.[34]

Notes

1. John Quincy Adams (hereafter JQA) to William Plumer, January 17, 1817, *Writings of John Quincy Adams*, ed. Worthington Chauncey Ford, 7 vols. (New York, 1913–1917), 6:140 (hereafter *Writings*).

2. JQA to Abigail Adams, May 16, 1817, ibid., 181.

3. JQA, diary entry, July 28, 1818, *Memoirs of John Quincy Adams: Comprising Portions of His Diary from 1795 to 1848*, ed. Charles Francis Adams, 12 vols. (Philadelphia, 1874–1877), 4:120 (hereafter *Memoirs*).

4. JQA to Alexander Hill Everett, December 29, 1817, *Writings*, 6:283.

5. JQA to James Monroe, February 8, 1816, ibid., 5:503; JQA to James Monroe, April 10, 1817, ibid., 6:175.

6. JQA, diary entry, April 16, 1817, *Memoirs*, 3:501.

7. JQA to Hyde de Neuville, September 24, 1817, *Writings*, 6:190; JQA to Elias Glenn, April 12, 1819, Department of State, Domestic Letters, Record Group 59, Microfilm 40, reel 15, National Archives, Washington, D.C.

8. JQA, diary entry, October 17, 1818, *Memoirs*, 4:134; JQA, diary entry, March 19, 1819, ibid., 308.

9. JQA, diary entry, December 30, 1817, ibid., 32; JQA, diary entry, December 6, 1817, ibid., 28.

10. JQA, diary entry, September 22, 1817, ibid., 9; JQA, diary entry, May 20, 1818, ibid., 98.

11. JQA to Abigail Adams, May 16, 1817, *Writings*, 6:181–82; JQA, diary entry, January 6, 1818, *Memoirs*, 4:36; JQA, diary entry, August 16, 1819, ibid., 411.

12. JQA to Richard Rush, May 20, 1818, *Writings*, 6:322; JQA to Benjamin Waterhouse, October 24, 1813, ibid., 4:526; JQA to John Adams, August 31, 1811, ibid., 209.

13. JQA, diary entry, September 21, 1817, *Memoirs*, 4:8.

14. JQA, diary entry, September 20, 1817, ibid.; JQA to Luis de Onís, March 12, 1818, Department of State, Notes to Foreign Ministers and Consuls in the United States, Record Group 59, Microfilm 38, reel 2, National Archives, Washington, D.C.

15. JQA to Alexander Hill Everett, December 29, 1817, *Writings*, 6:281; JQA, diary entry, March 24, 1818, *Memoirs*, 4:67.

16. James Monroe to John C. Calhoun, January 30, 1818, *Papers of John C. Calhoun*, ed. Robert L. Meriwether et al., 24 vols. to date (Columbia, S.C., 1959–), 2:104; Andrew Jackson to James Monroe, January 6, 1818, *Correspondence of Andrew Jackson*, ed. John Spencer Bassett, 7 vols. (Washington, D.C., 1926–1935), 2:345, 346.

17. JQA, diary entry, March 18, 1820, *Memoirs*, 5:25; JQA, diary entry, February 24, 1819, ibid., 4:278.

18. JQA to Thomas Boylston Adams, April 14, 1818, Adams Papers, Massachusetts Historical Society, Boston (microfilm), reel 145 (hereafter Adams Papers); JQA to John Adams, February 14, 1819, *Writings*, 6:530.

19. JQA, diary entry, March 18, 1820, *Memoirs*, 5:25; JQA, diary entry, January 3, 1819, ibid., 4:209; JQA, diary entry, December 28, 1818, ibid., 200; JQA, diary entry, March 18, 1820, ibid., 5:25.

20. JQA, diary entry, June 26, 1818, ibid., 4:103; JQA, diary entry, July 21, 1818, ibid., 115; JQA, diary entry, July 15, 1818, ibid., 108; JQA, diary entry, July 21, 1818, ibid., 115.

21. JQA to John Adams, February 14, 1819, *Writings*, 6:531; JQA, diary entry, November 28, 1818, *Memoirs*, 4:184; JQA, diary entry, January 2, 1819, ibid., 208.

22. JQA to Richard Rush, May 20, 1818, *Writings*, 6:321, 322.

23. JQA, diary entry, February 22, 1819, *Memoirs*, 4:274–75; JQA, diary entry, April 14, 1818, ibid., 79.

24. JQA, diary entry, "Day" [April 1819], Adams Papers, reel 6; JQA, diary entry, November 16, 1819, *Memoirs*, 4:439.

25. JQA, diary entry, January 2, 1820, *Memoirs*, 4:495.

26. JQA, diary entry, May 24, 1819, ibid., 370.

27. Henry Clay to Adam Beatty, January 22, 1820, *The Papers of Henry Clay*, ed. James F. Hopkins et al., 10 vols. and Supplement (Lexington, Ky., 1959–1992), 2:766; Henry Clay to Horace Holley, February 17, 1820, ibid., 781; Henry Clay to Jonathan Russell, January 29, 1820, ibid., 771; Henry Clay to Adam Beatty, January 22, 1820, ibid., 766.

28. JQA, diary entry, March 18, 1820, *Memoirs*, 5:26.

29. JQA, circular letter to Albert Gallatin, Richard Rush, and George W. Campbell, August 23, 1819, Department of State, Diplomatic Instructions, Record Group 59, Microfilm 77, reel 3, National Archives, Washington, D.C.; JQA, diary entry, March 25, 1820, *Memoirs*, 5:39; JQA, diary entry, March 31, 1820, ibid., 55.

30. JQA, diary entry, "Day" [May 1819], Adams Papers, reel 6; JQA, diary entry, March 18, 1819, *Memoirs*, 4:307; JQA, diary entry, March 3, 1821, ibid., 5:315; JQA, diary entry, June 4, 1819, ibid., 4:388.

31. JQA, diary entry, November 27, 1819, *Memoirs*, 4:453; JQA, diary entry, May 1, 1820, ibid., 5:84; JQA, diary entry, May 10, 1820, ibid., 109; JQA, diary entry, May 1, 1820, ibid., 84.

32. JQA, diary entry, May 11, 1820, ibid., 5:111; JQA, diary entry, December 3, 1819, ibid., 4:461.

33. JQA, diary entry, April 13, 1820, ibid., 5:68.

34. JQA, diary entry, February 14, 1821, ibid., 279; JQA, diary entry, March 3, 1821, ibid., 316.

4

A Frustrating World

1821–1825

To a far greater degree than one might expect, the beginning of James Monroe's second term as president—and, thus, of John Quincy Adams's second term as secretary of state—on March 4, 1821, coincided with significant changes in the problems facing American policymakers at home and abroad. A few days earlier, a final compromise of the Missouri Crisis had effectively ended two years of sectional jealousy and congressional paralysis. But, if the compromise had alleviated one source of domestic divisions, Monroe's reelection had intensified another, even though he had run unopposed and enjoyed nearly unanimous support in the electoral college. With the election of 1820 decided, attention turned immediately to the election of 1824, fueling new clashes between the leading candidates—Adams, Secretary of War John C. Calhoun, Secretary of the Treasury William H. Crawford, Speaker of the House Henry Clay, and, later, General Andrew Jackson. At the same time, the reratification of the Transcontinental Treaty ten days before Monroe's second inauguration had finally ended the long territorial dispute with Spain. But, by effectively settling the problems in the immediate neighborhood of the United States that had preoccupied policymakers since the War of 1812, it permitted, or even forced, Monroe and Adams to address a new set of problems that extended far beyond the union's borders. The regulation of foreign commerce, the suppression of the international slave trade, and the revolutions in Spanish America replaced Florida, Oregon, and Texas as critical issues during Adams's second term.

While Adams's basic goals remained the same during his second term, much else changed. He still accepted the importance and the difficulty of preserving peace. He still attempted to bring American foreign relations more fully under his own control. And he still worked for the commercial and, with greater hesitation, territorial expansion that he counted upon to strengthen the union. But he faced very different conditions and could claim far fewer successes after March 1821. The domestic divisions that were generated by the election campaign, while less threatening and less intense than those fueled by the Missouri Crisis and the Panic of 1819, continued to erode federal energy and involved Adams more directly. At the same time, the international issues that Adams confronted in his second term raised serious questions about established ideas and practices. These issues proved far less amenable to one of his preferred tactics—using the recognized weakness of the American government to disclaim responsibility for the actions of its citizens. More significant, Adams and other policymakers were forced to review and reconsider their underlying assumptions by deciding to what extent the thinking of the Founders remained relevant once most of the Western Hemisphere gained its independence. Facing such difficult challenges, Adams tried to shape policies that would advance both his personal interests and the national interest. He trusted that these goals were compatible; "it is no just cause of reproach to any man," he argued, "that in promoting to the utmost of his power the public good, he is desirous at the same time of promoting his own." During his second term, however, few of his policies achieved both of these goals.[1]

~

Throughout Adams's second term as secretary of state, the approaching presidential election of 1824 helped to establish the shifting domestic context for policymaking. Some jockeying for position had taken place among presidential hopefuls during the previous four years. But it was nothing like what began after Monroe's reelection and lasted through the final election of Adams by the House of Representatives in early 1825. The intensification of the contest created serious problems for Adams and the nation. Wanting to win the presidency very badly, Adams struggled between his republican belief that it should come to him through no effort of his own and his pragmatic recognition that it would not. He became increasingly preoccupied with the election to the detriment of his official business. With two other cabinet members also aspirants for the presidency, the whole administration suffered from frequently paralyzing internal divisions. These divisions spilled over into Congress, where each of the department secretaries, as well as the speaker of the House, had supporters. While the election of 1824 never had the same potential as the War of 1812 or the Missouri Crisis to destroy the union, the divisions it produced weakened federal power and authority at a time when major problems demanded attention and action.

By December 1818, less than halfway through Monroe's first term, Adams could already note in his diary that the "Government is, indeed, assuming daily more and more a character of cabal, and preparation, not for the next Presidential election, but for the one after." Monroe's administration had begun amidst widespread predictions of new political divisions. His landslide election in 1816 had clearly demonstrated the collapse of the Federalist party at the national level following the War of 1812. But the name "Era of Good Feelings" had not even been coined for this one-party period before political observers began warning of new divisions along either party or, more probably, personal lines. Adams shared this expectation. He quickly identified both Crawford—who had competed against Monroe for the Republican nomination in 1816—and Clay—who had wanted Monroe to name him secretary of state—as men whose presidential ambitions might lead them into opposition. Throughout Monroe's first term, Adams worried that Crawford or Clay wanted to find an issue that would inflame popular passions, divide the electorate, and provide the foundation for new parties that could advance their personal ambitions. No permanent new factions emerged in these years. But the Republicans who controlled the government still did not act with harmony and unanimity.[2]

As early as January 1820, Adams considered it "scarcely avoidable that [Monroe's] second term [would] be among the most stormy and violent" periods of American history. Monroe's second inauguration initiated a more public and more intense phase in the competition to succeed him. Throughout this process, Adams struggled against himself as much as against the other candidates. There is no question that he wanted to win the presidency. By the spring of 1824, he had convinced himself "that [he had] more at stake upon the result [of the election] than any other individual in the Union." And he clearly thought that his position as secretary of state made him the natural successor to Monroe since it had served as the route "to the head of the Executive" for each of the Republican

presidents. Still, he insisted that the presidency, of all public offices, "ought to be most freely and spontaneously bestowed" by
the people. Although well aware of the labors of the other candidates, Adams insisted to his supporters and to himself that he would
"do absolutely nothing" to advance his own chances. In fact, he
did quite a bit. He played some part in the decision of the Republicans in the Massachusetts state legislature to pass a resolution supporting his candidacy in February 1822. He tried to eliminate Clay
and Jackson as competitors by proposing them as ministers to Spanish American governments. He also explained his views on political matters in letters that he expected would be either circulated or
published and entered into a regular correspondence with a sup-
portive newspaper editor. Even Adams's frequent announcements
that he would not work on his own behalf served various purposes,
personal and political. They helped him to dispel any misgivings
that he might have had about his own actions. They allowed him
to position himself as the one candidate who would not stoop to
intrigue. And they even helped him to avoid the kind of personal
canvassing that would only have shown that, while he was "not
intentionally repulsive in [his] manners and deportment," he had
none of "the arts of a courtier" and "no powers of fascination."[3]

During Monroe's second term, the contest for the presidency
seriously affected policymaking, undermining the effectiveness of
the secretary of state, the executive branch, and the federal government. The campaign served to distract Adams from his work.
Even as he insisted that his "business was to serve the public to the
best of [his] abilities in the station assigned to [him], and not to
intrigue for further advancement," Adams, in fact, became increasingly preoccupied with the election. As it neared, his diary became
more and more an account of his own meetings with potential back-
ers and his competitors' efforts at "intrigue" and less and less a
record of the cabinet's critical discussions. He devoted precious time
to defending his reputation against attacks from politicians and
editors whom he viewed as proxies for the candidates. For example,
Adams spent much of the spring and summer of 1822 drafting and
revising newspaper essays, reviewing and compiling documents,
and, ultimately, assembling and editing a book in response to Congressman Jonathan Russell's charge that he had been willing to
abandon the interests of the West in order to advance those of New
England at Ghent. By early July, Adams confessed that "it [was] a
great mortification to [him] to have a large portion of the time which
ought to be devoted to the discharge of [his] public duties absorbed

in necessary self-defence." Still, he refused to let the matter rest, even after his friends assured him that Russell's charges had been entirely refuted. More than two months later, Adams was still preparing his *The Duplicate Letters, the Fisheries, and the Mississippi.*[4]

The campaign also served to distort Adams's perceptions of the positions taken by the other candidates on important policy questions. Adams might believe, as he noted in March 1820, that the "imputation of bad motives [was] one of the most envenomed weapons of political . . . controversy." Yet, he increasingly viewed his competitors for the presidency as so driven by their personal ambitions that they were willing to sacrifice the public good to advance their private interests. Accordingly, he became less willing to accept their proposals or credit their concerns when they differed from his own. He had long dismissed otherwise reasonable policy suggestions as politically motivated when they came from either Clay or Crawford. What changed over the course of Monroe's second term was his appraisal of Calhoun. As late as October 1821, Adams viewed Calhoun as "a man of fair and candid mind, of honorable principles, of clear and quick understanding, of cool self-possession, of enlarged philosophical views, and of ardent patriotism." But Adams also thought that Calhoun should abandon his presidential pretensions for a few years and support Adams's campaign. Once it became clear that Calhoun was not going to back his candidacy, Adams's thinking changed abruptly. By December 1823, Adams, as reported by one of his confidants, viewed Calhoun as a man without even "a root of principle," who "had been labouring incessantly to injure [Adams]" and who had suggested policies that "seemed designed expressly to make difficulty for the next President."[5]

The rival presidential aspirations of the principal cabinet members had effects that extended throughout the administration and were obvious to outsiders as well as insiders. Visiting the capital in February 1822, Clay noted the "divided Cabinet and distracted counsels" that stemmed from "*all* the prominent members of the Cabinet looking to the succession." A few months later, Adams described the cabinet as "nothing but a system of mining and countermining between Crawford and Calhoun to blow up each other." The presidential prospects of "*all* the candidates" except himself, as Adams saw it, unfortunately "depend[ed] upon the *failure* of the present Administration." Calhoun and Crawford attacked each other and, at least from Adams's perspective, joined forces to attack him. As a result, the Monroe administration offered few significant new policy proposals during its second term. In time, even the mundane business of running the executive branch fell hostage to the presidential campaign. Throughout his last year in office, Monroe essentially refused to propose any new nominations because of "the bearing which any appointment" that he might have made would have had "on the interests of the candidates." As Clay understood, the rivalry among the cabinet members had resulted in "a state of things extremely to be deprecated as it regards the public business."[6]

This rivalry did not affect only the executive branch, however. Over time, each of the presidential candidates built a group of supporters in Congress that either shared his principles or expected benefits from his success. Crawford and, not surprisingly, Clay proved especially adept at winning over congressmen. But Calhoun, Jackson, and even Adams eventually had their own blocs of regular supporters, despite Adams's assertion that he had "neither creature nor champion in either House." As a result, the policy conflicts that increasingly paralyzed the cabinet spilled over into the legislative branch. Congressmen divided over policy issues, with significant numbers working to defeat the administration on a wide range of major and minor issues. The most obvious area in which personal ambitions helped to influence policy decisions concerned military preparedness. A combination of republican principles, fiscal conservatism, and presidential aspirations led Crawford and his congressional supporters to reduce military expenditures by cutting the size of the army. Their target in this effort was Calhoun, whose candidacy depended entirely upon his management of the War Department. Their success had the effect of weakening American military power at a time when Monroe and Adams still saw grave dangers abroad.[7]

As early as May 1822, Adams feared "that this Administration [would] not hold together another year." The federal government seemed to be "at war with itself, both in the Executive, and between the Executive and the Legislature." While the administration did "hold together" for the rest of Monroe's presidency, the new political divisions that observers had been predicting since the War of 1812 deepened as the election neared. Difficult questions arose that demanded creative solutions during Monroe's second term. But the policymakers who were responsible for solving them were often distracted and divided. Within the federal government, within the cabinet, and even within the secretary of state, the election of 1824 fueled conflicts that sapped the energy needed to meet these new challenges at least as early as Monroe's second inauguration. Its effects intensified in the four years leading to an election that was so tightly contested that it had to be decided by the House of Representatives.[8]

~

Even as the approaching election produced a new context for policymaking at home, international developments presented a new set of issues to address abroad. By early March 1821, Adams had resolved in an acceptable, if not necessarily permanent, manner most of the problems in the immediate neighborhood of the United States. Doing so permitted, or even required, the administration to turn its attention to issues of a much larger scale. Some of these issues had lingered in the background during Adams's first term; others emerged anew as a result of ongoing developments in Europe and Spanish America. With Europe, most of Adams's policymaking after March 1821 concerned a variety of maritime questions. He resumed and expanded negotiations with France and Great Britain aimed at improving American access to foreign markets, both metropolitan and colonial. He also worked with the British to find an acceptable means for suppressing the international slave trade. And he drafted and proposed a convention to protect private property on the ocean in wartime. When he left the State Department for the President's Mansion in March 1825, Adams could point to few successes in any of these areas. He attributed his failure primarily to domestic opposition generated by the election campaign; there is no doubt that presidential rivalries were a factor. But Adams also failed, in part, because of his own errors. In these negotiations, he demanded too much, refused to make concessions, and overestimated his chances for success. Seeking policies that would protect the nation's interests without damaging his own prospects, Adams made little headway on these maritime issues.

Adams approached his commercial negotiations with France and Great Britain with goals that he traced back to the very infancy of the United States. What he wanted to secure from these powers emerged clearly from his analysis of why the United States could "really obtain nothing from Russia of any importance in a commercial treaty." Unlike France and Great Britain, Russia had "no discriminating duties [and] no colonial monopolies." "All the trade between us," Adams further noted, "is carried on in our vessels." By negotiating with France and Great Britain, he hoped, first, to open previously closed markets by removing the barriers to American trade with their colonies and, second, to eliminate existing trading disparities by establishing the principle of reciprocity. Reciprocity meant that each nation would charge the same fees and duties for foreign ships and goods as for its own ships and goods in its ports; as such, reciprocity would have produced even better trading terms than most-favored-nation status, which ultimately would have required each nation to treat all foreign ships and goods the same as each other, not the same as its own ships and goods. In Adams's view, such a "liberal principle of commercial intercourse with foreign nations was . . . one of the ingredients of our national independence [and had] originated with our national existence." Opening new colonial markets and, especially, ending discriminatory trade would benefit American farmers and merchants throughout the union. Adams saw his efforts on behalf of commercial expansion as "of the utmost importance to the welfare of the country."[9]

These commercial questions had received some consideration from Adams even during his first term. Immediately following the War of 1812, Congress had empowered the president to admit into American ports without additional fees or duties the ships of any nation that, whether by treaty or unilateral action, removed its discriminatory fees and duties against American ships. The same year, American and British diplomats in London, including Adams, had signed the Convention of 1815, providing for equal treatment in the ports of the United States and the British Isles. No such arrangement was concluded with France, which viewed its system of discriminatory duties as essential for securing a part of the trade to its own merchants. Hoping to force the British to extend reciprocity to its West Indian and North American colonies and the French to accept the principle at all, the administration tried to increase the pressure on its trading partners. In 1817 and 1818, Congress passed laws prohibiting, first, imports from British colonies except in American ships and, later, all imports from or exports to British colonies that were closed to American merchants, as most were. When the British opened Canadian ports to serve as entrepôts for their West Indian colonies, Congress responded in 1820 by closing American ports to all ships and goods from British colonies. The same year, it added a special duty to all French ships that traded in American ports; France retaliated by increasing the duties paid by American ships. As a result, Adams found the United States on the verge of trade wars with both Great Britain and France when he took up these maritime issues more fully after March 1821.

Often tense negotiations with France began in April 1821 and produced a commercial convention in June 1822. Adams could hardly claim this achievement as his own, however. As long as the United States insisted upon reciprocity and France demanded some degree of discrimination in its ports in favor of its own merchants, a resolution remained unattainable. Conversations with the French minister in Washington, Baron Guillaume Hyde de Neuville, and dispatches from the American minister in Paris, Albert Gallatin, suggested that the French would accept a fairly low level of discrimination and a plan to eliminate even these disparities over time. But the United States would have to concede the principle of reciprocity at least temporarily. The secretary of state repeatedly argued against such a concession in meetings with the French minister, the cabinet, and the president. "But, notwithstanding my argument," Adams recorded in his diary following one cabinet session, "it was determined that we should accept the basis of an unequal discrimination." He thought that the convention "surrender[ed]" a principle that "had formed the basis of our commercial policy" since the first days of American independence and predicted that it would "give great dissatisfaction here." Believing that he could have obtained a better arrangement, Adams blamed Crawford. Since "a bad Convention was precisely the thing suited to his interest," Crawford, in Adams's view, had "invariably been for conceding everything." Crawford—along with Gallatin, Calhoun, and Monroe—did, in fact, accept concessions. The resulting convention benefited American trade and eased Franco-American tensions.[10]

In the concurrent negotiations with Great Britain, Adams's unswerving commitment to the principles of reciprocity and open access prevented any resolution and produced a limited trade war that ultimately injured American commerce. Immediately after the War of 1812, the weakness of the United States and the likelihood of new conflicts on its borders had led to policies that were marked by patience and conciliation. The commercial conventions that Adams had helped to negotiate with the British in 1815 and 1818 embodied this approach, solving the easier problems—the direct trade between the United States and the British Isles—and postponing the harder ones—American access to British colonial markets. At the beginning of Adams's second term, progress on the latter issue seemed possible. Having wielded the stick of closed ports a year earlier, Congress offered the carrot of open trade in early 1821 when it authorized the president to reduce or remove most barriers to British ships and goods in exchange for relaxations in British restrictions on the colonial trade. In 1822, Parliament opened West Indian ports to American trade in certain products and under certain restrictions. But it insisted upon maintaining some discrimination in favor of ships and goods from the various parts of its empire; Canadian flour, for example, would pay lower duties than American flour. Monroe and Adams responded to Parliament's move in August 1824 with a proclamation reopening American ports to goods and ships from British colonies.

The proclamation did not waive the discriminatory duties paid by British ships coming from the colonies, however. As a result, it led to bitter feelings in Great Britain, tense discussions between Adams and the British minister in Washington, Stratford Canning, and, eventually, additional reprisals on both sides. Adams met Canning's initial complaints by reworking one of his favorite tactics from the past, searching for advantage in the very nature of a republican government. He insisted that "the principal and insuperable" obstacle to issuing another proclamation eliminating the discriminatory duties was simply "the want of authority in the Executive to remove them." Indeed, Congress clearly had not empowered the president to remove the duties, only to reopen the ports. It is equally clear, however, that Adams did not want either Congress or the president to remove them without further British concessions. He used the lack of authority to stall Canning over the fall of 1822, but did not suggest that Congress remove the duties when it met in December. Adams preferred, and the cabinet agreed, "that the regulation of the intercourse with the British Colonies [remain] a subject of negotiation between the Governments." Instead of asking Congress to eliminate the existing duties, he requested new ones that he hoped to wield to transform Great Britain's limited concession into the full and equal access to its colonies that would have matched his anticolonial ideals and strengthened his electoral chances. His demands, and the new pressures that he employed to achieve them, proved too extreme. He spent the rest of his term as secretary of state negotiating without results, while the British imposed retaliatory duties and, in 1826, closed the West Indian colonies entirely to American trade.[11]

Adams experienced even greater frustrations as a result of his simultaneous negotiations with Great Britain regarding the suppression of the international slave trade. The United States and Great

Britain had taken the lead in opposing the slave trade when each outlawed participation in the trade by its own citizens and importation of new slaves into its territories as of January 1808. Most European nations did not follow this lead. Either they refused to outlaw the trade at all or they failed to enforce their prohibitions effectively. Following the return of peace in Europe in 1815, the British cabinet tried to coordinate international action against the slave trade. Under the British plan, each nation would adopt laws barring its own subjects from participating in the trade and agree to allow the British navy to enforce these laws by stopping and searching its merchant ships. While this effort was directed at the European nations who had not acted vigorously against the slave trade, the British occasionally urged American policymakers to agree to a mutual, limited right of search in peacetime. Monroe and Adams certainly opposed the slave trade, believing that it deserved what Adams described as "the general indignation of mankind." And they occasionally offered to coordinate operations between American and British naval vessels on the coast of Africa. What they would not accept, as Adams repeatedly stated, were British searches of American vessels, which the federal government and the American people had so vigorously opposed in the context of impressment in the years before the War of 1812. Such searches, Adams asserted, were "not less odious to us than the slave-trade itself."[12]

If Adams had had his way, there would have been no Anglo-American discussion of the international slave trade at all in his second term. In early March 1821, he informed Canning that, since the administration's objections to the British plan were "insuperable," "it would henceforth be . . . agreeable to us not to be further urged" on the subject. Such inflexibility on the question of the right of search served both national interests—by reinforcing American opposition to impressment—and political ambitions—by displaying Adams's stand on a popular issue. Adams could imagine agreeing to a right of search in peacetime only if Great Britain would accept "an article, as strong and explicit as language can make it," foreswearing impressment from American ships in wartime. Congress was much more flexible. In May 1820, the House of Representatives had passed a resolution urging the president to negotiate toward "an entire and immediate abolition of the slave trade." In February 1823, it devised a way to accomplish this goal without actually surrendering the right of search. The key step was for each nation to agree that slave trading was a form of piracy. Under the law of nations, pirates were considered at war with all mankind; they could not claim protection from their own governments and could be captured by the ships of any nation. Redefined as pirates, slave traders could be searched and seized without giving offense to the nation whose flag they flew.[13]

With the House resolution both eliminating the "insuperable" obstacle to an agreement and demonstrating the popularity of more vigorous action, Adams initiated negotiations on the suppression of the slave trade through his minister in London, Richard Rush. Defining slave trading as piracy under the law of nations had not been Adams's idea. In his discussions in the cabinet and in his instructions to Rush, he left no doubt that he was trying "to carry into effect the resolution of the House of Representatives, and to meet the urgent pressure of the British Government." But he embraced the House's solution. He directed Rush not to offer any formal proposals until the British agreed to outlaw the slave trade as a form of piracy and drafted a convention based on this idea. At the same time, he took the opportunity to restate the government's, and his own, opposition to impressment and to secure the right of accused slave traders to trials in their own country. With the British government avid for an agreement, Rush easily concluded a convention in March 1824. As Adams noted, the final slave trade convention "varie[d] in very few and quite unimportant particulars" from his original draft. With the House resolution presumably providing evidence of public sentiment on this issue, the administration expected a quick ratification by the Senate.[14]

Instead, Monroe and Adams were "astonished" and "mortified" by the appearance of an anticonvention bloc in the Senate that, while unwilling to defeat the agreement entirely, attached a set of crippling amendments that ultimately made it unacceptable to Great Britain. Adams attributed this opposition to two sources— sectionalism and factionalism. With the British cabinet growing increasingly vocal in its hostility to slavery, southerners, he concluded, worried that an Anglo-American convention against "the slave-trade should turn [in]to a concert for the abolition of slavery." Adams more frequently looked to presidential ambitions to explain this "factious opposition" that had "so suddenly and unexpectedly gotten up to benefit Mr. Crawford by fastening odium upon me." Crawford's supporters in the Senate, ignoring the House resolution and the convention itself, accused Adams of conceding a right of search to the British that would encourage future impressment. Most political observers in Washington agreed with Adams that there was little substance to these charges. New York Senator Rufus King flatly attributed the opposition to the convention to "the presidential Election." In fact, factional divisions account for the votes on the amendments much better than sectional ones. On one key amendment, fifteen of the eighteen Crawfordites voted against twenty of the twenty-five non-Crawfordites, while northerners and southerners divided fairly evenly on each side.[15]

The Crawfordites certainly deserve much of the blame for the ultimate failure of the convention, but Adams made some critical errors as well. His accommodation to the redefinition of slave trading as piracy may have provided a handle for his political opponents, even though Crawford's allies in the House and, more galling to Adams, Crawford himself had initially backed the resolution. But Adams—as had so often been the case during his first term as secretary of state—had, in fact, made good use of that unexpected legislative intrusion in foreign policymaking. He had taken great pains in the convention to limit the right of search and to avoid any concession that might undermine future American arguments against British impressment. Adams's errors came elsewhere. In drafting the convention, he had not foreseen the impact of including the coast "of America" among the searchable areas, rather than limiting them to the coast of Africa and the high seas. The effect of this sweeping language was to rekindle memories of British ships lying off the coast to impress American sailors and raise concerns about British interference in the domestic slave trade between American ports. Furthermore, after the ratification, Adams failed to see that "the exception of the coast of America from the searchable seas" by a Senate amendment would lead Great Britain to reject the agreement. In his mind, "the essential bases of the Convention were untouched" by the amendments. The British, however, viewed a convention that did not allow their navy to search suspect vessels on the North or South American coasts as unworkable.[16]

In the summer of 1823, at the same time that he prepared new instructions for Rush concerning the British West Indies and the slave trade, Adams also proposed negotiations with Great Britain for "a Convention to regulate neutral and belligerent rights in time of war." His plan would have given noncontraband, private property—whether it was owned by a neutral or a belligerent and whether it was found on a neutral or belligerent merchant ship— almost total protection from seizure. In Adams's thinking, it would have meant "a great amelioration in the condition of man." Like reciprocity, Adams traced this extreme interpretation of "freedom of the seas" and neutral rights to the first days of American independence. And, like reciprocity, this idealistic position had little prospect of gaining widespread acceptance. Even as he tried to initiate Anglo-American negotiations on the subject, he admitted that he "had no hope it would now take root in England." Adams seems not to have realized, however, that his proposal was sure to be opposed not only in Europe but also at home. The United States had always argued for the broadest interpretation of neutral rights; expecting to remain neutral in most European wars, such a position would benefit American merchants and producers. But the War of 1812 had shown that, when the United States did go to war, its most effective maritime weapon would be privateers who could capture the enemy's merchant ships; Adams's convention would have abandoned this weapon. He correctly predicted that the British would not accept this radical position in 1823, but did not understand that neither would his countrymen. When the major powers of Europe did adopt a declaration based on Adams's position in 1856, the United States refused to join them by foreswearing privateering.[17]

Adams devoted a good deal of time and energy to a variety of maritime issues during his second term as secretary of state, but achieved few successes. His proposal for a convention to protect private property at sea in wartime died without ever becoming a subject of formal negotiation. The slave trade convention, as revised by the Senate amendments, evaporated when the British refused to ratify. His commercial pressures on Great Britain led not to open access to colonial markets, but to new reprisals that damaged American commerce, and Adams's political position, during his presidency. Only in the case of France had commercial problems been solved, but it was only the rejection of Adams's policies by Monroe that had made a solution possible. Given the success of Adams's first term, how can we account for the failure of these years? For one thing, these maritime questions differed greatly from the earlier territorial issues; they had a more direct impact on European interests and had to be settled with a strong Great Britain and France rather than a weak Spain. At the same time, Adams faced more effective domestic opposition fueled by the intensified presidential rivalries. But Adams also lacked the flexibility and creativity of earlier years. Reluctant to give his political rivals a weapon to use against him, Adams clung stubbornly to what he believed to be popular positions on such principles as reciprocity, open access, the right of search, and freedom of the seas. Adhering to these principles would serve the nation's long-term interests as well as his current political ambitions. But compromising on them, as he had earlier compromised on his territorial aspirations by abandoning the claim to Texas, might have better served the nation's short-term interests and produced more successes.

~

Even as he devoted more time to maritime issues with Europe during his second term as secretary of state, Adams also focused more attention on changing conditions in the Western Hemisphere. American policymakers had closely followed and carefully responded to revolutionary upheaval in Spanish America for more than a decade before March 1821. In general, especially after the War of 1812, their response had been determined more by conditions on their borders and in Europe than by developments in Spanish America. The final ratification of the Transcontinental Treaty in February 1821 made it possible for Monroe and Adams to reevaluate these developments and rethink their policies. What they discovered proved deeply unsettling to them. By the fall of 1821, the revolutionaries had defeated Spanish troops and toppled Spanish authority in all of the mainland colonies. The emergence of independent nations in Spanish America simultaneously reinvigorated and threatened the original logic of the Founders. For the first time, American policymakers had to address the situation that the Founders had feared—the existence of a multitude of independent nations in the Western Hemisphere. Monroe and Adams responded by encouraging the new Spanish American nations to adopt political, diplomatic, and commercial principles that they believed would promote peace and prosperity in the New World. When they faced a European challenge to their goal of an independent, republican New World in the fall of 1823, they tried to counter it with what would later be called the Monroe Doctrine. Their efforts did not meet even their short-term goals and left unresolved the long-term question of how to react to the radical changes in the Western Hemisphere.

Though it was subsequently a subject of frequent debate and controversy, American policy toward the Spanish American revolutions was established, at least in general terms, shortly after the War of 1812. Uncertain about the actual state of Spanish America, convinced of the inveterate hostility of the European powers (particularly the Holy Alliance of Russia, Spain, Austria, and France), and alarmed by the demonstrated weakness of the United States, the Madison administration had crafted a policy of neutrality in the conflict between Spain and its colonies. As defined by the administration, neutrality did allow trading with both parties, but did not include recognizing the independence of the colonies if that risked embroiling the United States in a war with Spain and possibly other European nations. Monroe and Adams continued this cautious approach, even though they often differed over whether they could eliminate the dangers by coordinating recognition with Great Britain, France, and Russia. Once they learned in November 1819 that the fate of the Transcontinental Treaty was entangled with the question of recognition, Monroe and Adams became even more reluctant to act. Over the next fourteen months, recognition remained a hostage to the uncertain fate of the treaty.

The final ratification of the treaty in February 1821 did not ensure a change of policy, however. In a meeting with Clay in March 1821, Adams "acknowledge[d that] nothing had hitherto occurred to weaken in [his] mind the view which [he] had taken of this subject from the first." He "had never doubted" that the end result of the struggle would be the "entire independence" of the Spanish Americans. But he did not expect them to "establish free or liberal institutions of government." He argued that the United States must remain neutral, which in his view, unlike Clay's, did not yet allow for recognition. "The principle of neutrality to *all* foreign wars was," he believed, "fundamental to the continuance of our liberties and of our Union." This fierce commitment to neutrality appeared publicly in the Fourth of July oration that Adams delivered, at the request of Congress, in the Capitol four months later. Adams predicted that the principles of the Declaration of Independence would move the people to rise against tyranny in the future in Europe, as at present in South America. In these anticolonial and antimonarchical struggles, the United States would be "the well-wisher to the freedom and independence of all." But, he insisted, it should "[go] not abroad in search of monsters to destroy"; "by once enlisting under other banners than her own," the United States would find itself drawn into countless wars. In time, its own "freedom and independence" would be imperiled as it embarked upon a career of "dominion and power." Such a powerful and public statement of noninterventionist principles left little room for Monroe and Adams to risk recognizing the Spanish American nations as long as their struggle against Spain continued.[18]

Within a year of Adams's conversation with Clay and Fourth of July oration, however, the administration, encouraged by the secretary of state, decided to recognize Buenos Aires, Chile, Colombia, Mexico, and Peru—all of Spain's mainland colonies. Monroe and Adams abandoned their old opposition to recognition without abandoning their old concerns. They still found few signs of political stability or republican government among the Spanish Americans; in fact, there was new evidence that some of the rebel colonies might agree to import a minor European prince as a king if that would help to reconcile Spain to their independence. Monroe and Adams still worried, moreover, about the hostility of the European powers, who forcibly overthrew the republican government of Naples in early 1821. Writing to Adams that July, Monroe asserted that the United States had "much to apprehend from the hostile feeling of many of the sovereigns of Europe towards us"; "war with them," he calculated, "is not an improbable event." Finally, Monroe and Adams still accepted that the United States could not risk a war. The Missouri Crisis, the Panic of 1819, and the election campaign had badly divided the people and the government; even more important, the reduction in federal revenues resulting from the Panic had given Crawford's supporters in Congress the votes that they needed to cut the army and navy. What had changed by early 1822 that made possible a new policy was not the conditions that had always weighed against recognition, but the character of the contest between Spain and its colonies. By November 1821, new reports from Central and South America, particularly Peru and Mexico, had convinced Adams that "the Spanish authorities [were] falling away in every part of that continent."[19]

Monroe and Adams now faced a dramatically altered situation. From their perspective, the United States had suddenly gained five indisputably independent neighbors in the Western Hemisphere with necessarily conflicting interests. All of the fears that the Founders had expressed in the 1780s when they predicted disunion in North America were revived on a much larger scale in the early 1820s. Applying the logic of the Founders, Monroe and Adams believed that an independent New World might develop in one of two ways. The new Spanish American nations might fall under the control, formal or informal, of the European powers. The New World would become merely an extension of the European balance of power, involving its nations in Europe's wars and surrounding the United States with hostile monarchies. Or the Spanish American states might retain their independence and behave like any sovereign nation. As such, they would use commercial regulations and military forces to compete with each other and with the United States for land, trade, and influence. Monroe and Adams deemed neither of these prospects compatible with American interests. In either case, the United States would have to seek foreign alliances, adopt a more centralized—and, thus, less republican—government, and accept new limits on its trade and expansion. The goals of the Revolution—goals that had been secured and advanced for three decades by the American union—seemed to be in jeopardy.

The administration responded to these concerns in the first weeks of 1822 by deciding to extend formal diplomatic recognition to five Spanish American nations. None of the earlier obstacles to recognition had disappeared, but now Monroe and Adams had to weigh the long-term threat of an independent New World against the immediate risk of a war with Spain and possibly other European powers. As Monroe understood, under these conditions, there was "*danger* in standing *still* or moving *forward*." In early 1822, Monroe and Adams concluded that the long-term threat of "standing *still*" was more important. They hoped that, by recognizing the new states before any other nation, they could shape the Western Hemisphere's emerging political system into the form that best suited American interests. Opening formal relations with the new states would enable Monroe and Adams to promote throughout Spanish America the diplomatic, political, and commercial principles of the United States. The new nations would be encouraged to model themselves upon their northern neighbor—distancing themselves from European affairs, organizing themselves into weak republican governments, and committing themselves to liberal principles of neutral rights and open commerce. If the Spanish American states adopted this model, they would limit the means through which they could promote their interests, just as the United States had. As a result, they would be less dangerous neighbors. Monroe and Adams trusted that the general adoption of these principles would benefit the new states as well as the United States, even though it would only ameliorate, rather than eliminate, the inherent dangers of competition between sovereign neighbors.[20]

When the administration finally sent its first ministers to the new states—Caesar A. Rodney to Buenos Aires and Richard C. Anderson to Colombia—a year later, Adams prepared their initial instructions with these goals in mind. He fully appreciated the importance of his work, informing Monroe that "the foundations of the future permanent intercourse political and commercial between the United States and the new Spanish American nations must be laid in the instructions for these diplomatic missions." These foundations would rest on what Adams saw as the shared interest of the United States and the Spanish American states "that they should all be governed by republican institutions, politically and commercially independent of Europe." Republican government, diplomatic isolation from Europe, and liberal commerce would be pressed upon Spanish America in order to secure independence, republicanism, and prosperity in the United States. Rodney and Anderson were directed to discourage the Spanish Americans from forming any connections with the European powers since such ties were "always connected with systems of subserviency to *European* interests." At the same time, they were to encourage their hosts to adopt written constitutions that protected individual rights and subordinated military to civilian rule. Finally, they were to urge the new states to sign commercial treaties that included at least most-favored-nation status, if not reciprocity, and that asserted a broad view of neutral rights. Adams had no doubt that it was for the welfare of "our sisters of the southern continent . . . , no less than for that of the world, that they should found themselves" from the beginning upon "the principles upon which *our* confederated republic is founded."[21]

The same thinking that produced the decision to recognize in the winter of 1822 and that shaped the first set of instructions in the spring of 1823 determined the administration's response to a new crisis that fall. In October, the administration learned that France, Russia, and Austria—having invaded Spain to topple the constitutional government and restore the king the preceding spring—intended to assist Spain in regaining control of its colonies. This information came from Rush in London, along with a British proposal for a joint statement in which the two powers would declare their opposition to outside interference in Spanish America and disavow any intention of acquiring territory from Spain's empire. Adams received confirmation of Rush's news about the plans of the Holy Alliance from the Russian minister in Washington, Baron Hendrik de Tuyll van Serooskerken. The crisis raised two interconnected questions for the administration. How should it react to the Holy Alliance's threat to the Spanish American states? And how should it respond to Great Britain's proposal for a joint statement? In the month before Congress met in early December, the cabinet discussed these questions at great length. Monroe, Adams, and the other cabinet members did not entirely agree about the developing situation or the appropriate response. Adams tended to see less danger of an Allied invasion and more peril from the British proposal than the president or the secretary of war, for example. But all could agree that it was precisely because they had recognized the Spanish American nations and had committed the United States to an independent, republican New World that they needed to respond at all.

Working from the logic of the earlier decision to recognize the Spanish American states, the administration believed that the United States had to check the Allied threat and that it had to try, at least, to do so without accepting the British proposal. In reconceptualizing the New World at the time of recognition, Monroe and Adams had defined new interests for the United States. In doing so, they had also identified new ways in which it could be threatened by Europe. Intervention by the Holy Alliance in Spanish America would revive all of the dangers that recognition had been intended to remove. Even if the Allied effort to restore Spanish authority ultimately failed, and Adams always believed that it would, the attempt itself seemed certain to undermine American goals in the region. Within each state, loyalists and monarchists would gain strength, while military leaders would retain power that should have been surrendered to civilian governments. The Allies would eventually abandon their effort to restore Spanish control, but Adams feared that they would then seek dominion for themselves. "The ultimate result of their undertaking," he predicted to the cabinet, "would be to recolonize [the new states], partitioned out among themselves." With France established in Buenos Aires and Mexico and Russia entrenched in Peru, Chile, and California, the administration's worst fears would be realized.[22]

From the beginning of the cabinet debates, Monroe and Adams looked for ways to check the Holy Alliance without accepting the British proposal. "The President," Adams noted in his diary, "was averse to any course which should have the appearance of taking a position subordinate to that of Great Britain." Adams certainly agreed. In an oft-quoted statement, he asserted that "it would be more candid, as well as more dignified, to avow our principles explicitly to Russia and France, than to come in as a cock-boat in the wake of the British man-of-war." But Monroe and Adams were not merely looking for a way to maintain appearances. On one hand, because Great Britain had not yet recognized the new states, it was not committed to their independence as the United States was. Without such a common commitment, Adams worried that any joint statement would "[rest] only upon a casual coincidence of interests" that would leave the British free to change their policy whenever they wished. On the other hand, Monroe and Adams calculated that, by acting alone, the United States could thwart the plans of the Holy Alliance and enhance its own influence in Spanish America. Unilateral action, in Monroe's thinking, would have a "better effect with our southern neighbours, as well as with Russia & other allied powers." Believing that Russia, in particular, feared Anglo-American cooperation, the administration would hold out to the Holy Alliance the possibility of preventing it simply by abandoning the Spanish American invasion. By checking the Allied threat without British support, Monroe and Adams would also help to prevent the spread of British influence in the new states. The alternative of following Great Britain's lead or, worse yet, allowing it to act alone, Adams warned, "would throw them completely into her arms, and . . . make them her Colonies instead of those of Spain."[23]

Almost immediately, Adams concluded that this crisis had to be met with a multifaceted, but coordinated, response. After the first cabinet discussion of this matter, he informed Monroe that the instructions to Rush addressing the British proposal and the reply to de Tuyll, as well as new instructions for the ministers in Russia and France, "must all be parts of a combined system of policy and adapted to each other." Monroe, Adams noted, "fully concurred." Eventually, the elements of this "combined system of policy" included as well instructions for the new minister to Chile, meetings with the Colombian minister in Washington, and the dispatching of a secret agent to Europe. The most public facet of this response, at the time, and the most significant, subsequently, however, was the president's annual message to Congress. In time, the three paragraphs from the message that dealt with this crisis would be known as the Monroe Doctrine. They asserted three crucial principles that derived from the administration's new appraisal of the United States's hemispheric interests. The first informed the European powers, especially Great Britain and Russia, that the Western Hemisphere was no longer open to new colonization. The second addressed the current crisis directly by warning the Allies that the United States would view "any attempt on their part to extend their system to any portion of this hemisphere as dangerous to our peace and safety." The third reaffirmed that the United States would not involve itself in Europe's "internal concerns." With this message, the administration publicly took a bold, unilateral stand against the Holy Alliance, "mak[ing] an American cause," as Adams wished, "and adher[ing] inflexibly to [it]."²⁴

At home, this bold stand received widespread praise. Public meetings, private letters, and newspaper editorials all tended to support the forcefulness of the administration's public position. Both houses of Congress quickly sought ways to "[echo] back the Sentiments of the President's message" through resolutions. On the evening that the message was sent to Congress, Adams sought out Clay's opinion. Though they had usually battled over Spanish American policy during the preceding six years, the speaker of the House informed the secretary of state that he strongly approved of the administration's publicly expressed willingness to resist the Holy Alliance's threatened invasion. Two months later, he moved a resolution in the House that would have placed Congress squarely behind this policy. It was not just at home, moreover, that Monroe's message sparked such favorable comments. Among European liberals and Spanish American revolutionaries, it was immediately celebrated for its republican sentiments and its diplomatic stance. "The manly message of the President of the U.S. and the spirited feeling of the people at large and their representatives," the Marquis de Lafayette apprised Adams from France, "have produced an admirable and timely impression" in Europe.²⁵

But Monroe's annual message can be understood only in the context of the other elements of the administration's "combined system of policy." Taking all of its elements together, this policy was more tentative and more flexible than the message alone would suggest. The instructions for the new minister to France, for example, directed him to explain the message to his hosts, but warned him to "avoid any measure by which the Government might be prematurely implicated." The instructions for Rush made perfectly clear the administration's, particularly the president's, desire to keep open its options. As Adams drafted these instructions, Monroe insisted that they preserve even the possibility of accepting the original British proposal for a joint statement. If the crisis deepened despite the position taken publicly in the message and privately through diplomacy, Monroe reasoned, a joint statement, however unappealing in the abstract, might offer the only means of preventing an Allied invasion of Spanish America. Even after they received dispatches from London and Paris in late December reporting that a series of Anglo-French meetings had defused the crisis, Monroe and Adams watched Europe closely, prepared to revise their stand as necessary. "The policy of Great Britain & of Continental Europe, with regard to South America," Adams argued as late as May 1824, "is not yet fully disclosed." Monroe and Adams continued to await new developments and remained ready "to adapt our own measures in reference to them."[26]

The limits to the administration's position, as publicly and boldly stated in the president's message, emerged clearly in the months after its publication. The most important of these limits had been present from the beginning. Even though the message had warned that the United States would view any interference by the Holy Alliance in the affairs of the Spanish American states "as the manifestation of an unfriendly disposition toward [itself]," the administration had never intended to support its words with force, at least not if it had to act alone. "It does not follow, from what has been said," Monroe insisted in early December 1823, "that we should be bound to engage in war," particularly if Great Britain remained neutral. Monroe and Adams always realized that, if the Holy Alliance persisted with its plans, they might have to retreat from their unilateral stand; they prepared their instructions to keep open their options for such a contingency. Because British diplomacy had checked the Allied threat before the message reached Europe (in fact, before it was even written), the limits to the administration's public position were exposed not by the response of the European powers, but by the reaction of the Spanish American states. In a way that Monroe and Adams had never imagined, some of the Spanish American states embraced the message. In July 1824, the Colombian minister asked the administration to fulfill its stated principles by signing an alliance and supporting his country against French pressures. Monroe and Adams refused. Trying to cover their retreat, Adams explained that the message addressed only "a deliberate and concerted system of the allied Powers to exercise force." Even in that case, the administration would act only with the support of Congress and "a previous understanding" with Great Britain.[27]

The Monroe Doctrine's greater immediate impact was upon an ongoing territorial dispute over the Pacific Northwest. Four powers had claims in this region when Adams entered office in 1817. Spain's (which became Mexico's) had been limited to south of the 42nd parallel by the Transcontinental Treaty; the United States and Great Britain had agreed to joint occupation of their claims for a period of ten years in the Convention of 1818. But Russian pretensions remained unlimited and undefined. In the fall of 1821, the czar tried to strengthen his position by issuing a ukase closing both coasts and the waters of the Pacific north of 51° north latitude to foreigners. Adams immediately protested, but the limits of the respective Russian, British, and American claims remained undetermined. In the spring and summer of 1823, Adams worked to repel advancing Russian claims that seemed likely to push British claims further south. He hoped for a tripartite convention, to last for ten years, that would permit navigation, fishing, and commerce in any unoccupied areas of the coast while limiting Russian settlement to north of 55°, American settlement to south of 51°, and British settlement to the area in between. Such negotiations would almost certainly have failed in the face of a British insistence upon the freedom to settle as far north as 57° and as far south as the Columbia River. The Monroe Doctrine—by rebuffing the British proposal of a united stand against the Holy Alliance and asserting American opposition to new colonization in the New World—led the British to excuse themselves from these talks. In April 1824, the United States and Russia easily concluded a convention in St. Petersburg that included much that Adams sought, though it shifted the limit of Russian settlement south to 54°40'.

The final collapse of Spain's continental empire during the early 1820s posed significant challenges for Monroe and Adams; in the short-term, at least, their responses failed to achieve their goals. The ultimate success of the Spanish American revolutions held tremendous promise—opening new markets for American trade and, in Adams's thinking, rendering it "impossible that the old exclusive and excluding Colonial system should much longer endure anywhere." But it also reinvigorated the fears about how neighboring sovereignties interact with each other—and how such interactions could endanger the goals of the American Revolution— that had led the Founders to construct "a more perfect union" in the 1780s. Monroe and Adams responded to this challenge by trying to promote throughout the New World the principles that they trusted would ease competition between its states. They looked to recognition itself to begin this process. Its early effects were not encouraging. Nine months after recognition was announced, Adams "observed that those countries were yet all in a convulsive and revolutionary state." Faced with a new external challenge to their efforts in Spanish America a year later, Monroe and Adams stayed true to their new assessment of American interests, devising a set of measures that could check an Allied invasion without expanding British influence or risking an unwelcome war. But, although the Monroe Doctrine acquired tremendous significance in American policymaking eventually, it had no impact upon the crisis it was written to address. With the crisis resolved by Anglo-French diplomacy, Monroe and Adams quickly retreated from the message's implications.[28]

~

Adams's tenure as secretary of state ended in early March 1825 at a time of both personal success and national well-being. After four years of difficult campaigning prior to the election and two months of anxious waiting before its outcome was settled by the House of Representatives, Adams won the presidency, fulfilling his own and his parents' early expectations. At the same time, the condition of the country as a whole had improved markedly. "There never has been a period of more tranquillity at home and abroad since our existence as a nation than that which now prevails," Adams recorded in late November 1824. Despite the continued uncertainty surrounding the election, this judgment was correct; there was clearly nothing happening in late 1824 and early 1825 that compared to the repeated internal and international crises of the previous half-century. Admitting that Monroe's presidency ended in an era of "tranquillity" should not obscure the fact that very few of Adams's policies of the preceding four years had actually achieved their goals. In his maritime negotiations with Great Britain and France, Adams labored, generally unsuccessfully, to balance personal ambitions and national interests. In his multifaceted response to Spanish American independence, he confronted developments that struck at the very foundations of his, and the Founders', understanding of American security and American interests. As president for four years after March 1825, Adams continued to struggle with these challenges.[29]

Notes

1. John Quincy Adams (hereafter JQA), diary entry, March 4, 1820, *Memoirs of John Quincy Adams: Comprising Portions of His Diary from 1795 to 1848*, ed. Charles Francis Adams, 12 vols. (Philadelphia, 1874–1877), 5:13 (hereafter *Memoirs*).

2. JQA, diary entry, December 17, 1818, ibid., 4:193.

3. JQA, diary entry, January 8, 1820, ibid., 497; JQA, diary entry, May 8, 1824, ibid., 6:324; JQA, diary entry, March 13, 1819, ibid., 4:297; JQA, diary entry, March 18, 1818, ibid., 64; JQA to Louisa Catherine Adams, August 11, 1821, *Writings of John Quincy Adams*, ed. Worthington Chauncey Ford, 7 vols. (New York, 1913–1917), 7:170–71 (hereafter *Writings*).

4. JQA, diary entry, March 18, 1818, *Memoirs*, 4:64; JQA, diary entry, July 1, 1822, ibid., 6:40.

5. JQA, diary entry, March 4, 1820, ibid., 5:13; JQA, diary entry, October 15, 1821, ibid., 361; William Plumer Jr. to William Plumer, December 3, 1823, *The Missouri Compromises and Presidential Politics, 1820–1825: From the Letters of William Plumer, Junior, Representative from New Hampshire*, ed. Everett Somerville Brown (St. Louis, 1926), 86, 87.

6. Henry Clay to Unknown Recipient, February 26, 1822, *The Papers of Henry Clay*, ed. James F. Hopkins et al., 10 vols. and Supplement (Lexington, Ky., 1959–1992), Supplement:101 (hereafter *Papers of Clay*); JQA, diary entry, May 9, 1822, *Memoirs*, 5:525; JQA, diary entry, March 3, 1821, ibid., 315; James Monroe to John Taylor, February 9, 1824, Worthington C. Ford, ed., "Letters of James Monroe, 1790–1827," *Proceedings of the Massachusetts Historical Society* 3d ser., 42 (May 1909): 338; Henry Clay to Unknown Recipient, February 26, 1822, *Papers of Clay*, Supplement:101.

7. JQA, diary entry, May 9, 1822, *Memoirs*, 5:525.

8. JQA, diary entry, April 14, 1822, ibid., 490.

9. JQA, diary entry, November 29, 1821, ibid., 430; JQA, diary entry, November 28, 1821, ibid., 427.

10. JQA, diary entry, May 24, 1821, ibid., 354, 353; JQA, diary entry, June 21, 1822, ibid., 6:27.

11. JQA, diary entry, October 30, 1822, ibid., 6:92; JQA, diary entry, November 8, 1822, ibid., 97.

12. JQA to Richard Rush, February 6, 1821, *Writings*, 7:94, 92 n. 1.

13. JQA, diary entry, March 7, 1821, *Memoirs*, 5:321; JQA, diary entry, December 4, 1821, ibid., 448; House Resolution, May 12, 1820, *Annals of Congress*, 16th Cong., 1st sess., 2236.

14. JQA, diary entry, June 20, 1823, *Memoirs*, 6:150–51; JQA, diary entry, April 28, 1824, ibid., 310.

15. JQA, diary entry, May 18, 1824, ibid., 338; JQA, diary entry, May 14, 1824, ibid., 330; JQA, diary entry, May 12, 1824, ibid., 328; JQA, diary entry, May 27, 1824, ibid., 362; Rufus King to C. King, May 22, 1824, *The Life and Correspondence of Rufus King: Comprising His Letters, Private and Official, His Public Documents and His Speeches*, ed. Charles R. King, 6 vols. (New York, 1894–1900), 6:571. Political loyalties in Congress at the time of the slave trade convention vote were determined using Kenneth C. Martis, *The Historical Atlas of Political Parties in the United States Congress, 1789–1989* (New York, 1989), 87. I am indebted to S. Heath Mitton for sharing his calculations and analysis of the slave trade convention votes with me; his dissertation will show that the voting breakdown was too complicated to be accounted for, in full, by either factional or sectional loyalties alone.

16. JQA, diary entry, May 23, 1824, *Memoirs*, 6:350.

17. JQA, diary entry, July 28, 1823, ibid., 164.

18. JQA, diary entry, March 9, 1821, ibid., 5:324–25; JQA, "Mr. Adams' Oration," *Niles' Weekly Register* 20 (July 21, 1821): 331.

19. James Monroe to JQA, July 24, 1821, *Writings*, 7:138 n. 2; JQA, diary entry, November 13, 1821, Adams Papers, Massachusetts Historical Society, Boston (microfilm), reel 35 (hereafter Adams Papers).

20. James Monroe to Thomas Jefferson, March 14, 1822, *The Writings of James Monroe: Including a Collection of His Public and Private Papers and*

Correspondence Now for the First Time Printed, ed. Stanislaus Murray Hamilton, 7 vols. (New York, 1898–1903), 6:213 (hereafter *Writings of Monroe*).

21. JQA to James Monroe, May 10, 1823, *Writings*, 7:423; JQA to Caesar Augustus Rodney, May 17, 1823, ibid., 429, 432; JQA to Richard C. Anderson, May 27, 1823, ibid., 468–69.

22. JQA, diary entry, November 26, 1823, *Memoirs*, 6:207.

23. JQA, diary entry, November 7, 1823, ibid., 178, 179; JQA to Richard Rush, November 30, 1823, *Diplomatic Correspondence of the United States Concerning the Independence of the Latin-American Nations*, ed. William R. Manning, 3 vols. (Washington, D.C., 1925), 1:215 (hereafter *Diplomatic Correspondence*); James Monroe to James Madison, December 20, 1823, James Madison Papers, Library of Congress, Washington, D.C. (microfilm), reel 26; JQA, diary entry, November 26, 1823, *Memoirs*, 6:208.

24. JQA, diary entry, November 7, 1823, *Memoirs*, 6:179; James Monroe, "Seventh Annual Message," December 2, 1823, *A Compilation of the Messages and Papers of the Presidents, 1789–1897*, comp. James D. Richardson, 10 vols. (Washington, D.C., 1897–1899), 2:218, 219 (hereafter *Messages of the Presidents*); JQA, diary entry, November 22, 1823, *Memoirs*, 6:198.

25. JQA, diary entry, December 23, 1823, Adams Papers, reel 38; Marquis de Lafayette to JQA, January 24, 1824, ibid., reel 464.

26. JQA to James Brown, December 23, 1823, *Diplomatic Correspondence*, 1:221; JQA to Henry A. S. Dearborn, May 11, 1824, Adams Papers, reel 147.

27. James Monroe, "Seventh Annual Message," December 2, 1823, *Messages of the Presidents*, 2:218; James Monroe to Thomas Jefferson, December 1823, *Writings of Monroe*, 6:345; JQA to José María Salazar, August 6, 1824, *Diplomatic Correspondence*, 1:226.

28. JQA, diary entry, November 25, 1822, *Memoirs*, 6:104; JQA, diary entry, November 28, 1822, ibid., 110.

29. JQA, diary entry, November 30, 1824, ibid., 432.

5

A Troubled Presidency

1825–1829

Even the strongest proponents of the idea that John Quincy Adams was "the nation's greatest secretary of state" generally admit that "he was also one of its least successful presidents." He entered office in March 1825 in the weakest position of any president before or since, having been elected by the House of Representatives without having received even a plurality of either the popular or the electoral vote. Overwhelmingly defeated by Andrew Jackson in the election of 1828, Adams left office in March 1829 as only the second president to serve just one term (his father had been the first). His presidency brought a steady stream of diplomatic frustration and domestic failure, resulting in a serious personal depression. Shortly after leaving office in March 1829, his secretary of state, Henry Clay, labored to convince the public of the recent administration's achievements in a series of speeches. At home, he reminded one audience, the nation was "in the highest state of prosperity"; all of its "great domestic interests [had] been fostered and improved" by the administration. Abroad, "the honor and the rights of the nation [had] been maintained" and there was not even "a speck of war on the political horizon." All that Clay said was correct. But Adams himself saw, and knew that people would later emphasize, instead, "the overwhelming ruin of the Administration."[1]

Adams certainly had not expected such failure when he became president in the spring of 1825. He had realized, as he noted in his inaugural address, that he assumed his new duties "less possessed of [the public's] confidence in advance than any of [his] predecessors."

Nonetheless, he had confidently predicted success. Within a few months of entering office, Adams and his cabinet crafted and, whenever possible, launched a sweeping program of domestic and foreign policies. These interconnected measures showed clearly the impact upon Adams of the ideas of the Founders, the lessons of the Embargo and the War of 1812, and the logic of the Monroe administration's response to Spanish American independence. With the executive directly under his control for the first time and Congress apparently still under the sway of his secretary of state, Adams seemingly had solid grounds to predict success. Instead, in most cases, he found failure. The reasons for these failures were many and varied. He continued to struggle with some of the obstacles that had hampered his efforts during the preceding eight years. More significant, he faced vehement and potent opposition at home as a new Democratic party coalesced around a personal and political hostility to Adams; the resignation apparent in his response to this political situation further undermined his efforts. As important as these factors may have been, however, the source of many of the new administration's problems was the president himself. Adams's concerns and goals—the concerns and goals that he had inherited from the Founders—could not easily be applied to conditions, at home and abroad, that had changed dramatically between the 1780s and the 1820s. As he tried to adjust his measures to these new conditions, Adams often exacerbated the problems that he sought to solve.[2]

~

For Adams, election to the presidency both consummated the personal goals that his parents had set for him in his youth and promised to advance the political goals that he had identified for the nation since the 1790s. As soon as he knew the final outcome of the vote in the House, Adams signalled his awareness that the election reflected upon his parents as well as himself by sending a brief note "offer[ing his] congratulations" to his father on "the event of this day." He entered office three weeks later committed to using the opportunity that his parents' early guidance, his own diligent efforts, and the people's and the House's votes had provided him to benefit the nation. His inaugural address showed clearly that Adams viewed himself as responsible for preserving the accomplishments of the Founders and of his predecessors "as a precious inheritance" that had "secured the freedom and happiness of this people" "to an extent far beyond the ordinary lot of humanity." Adams expected the federal government to use its energy, at home and abroad, to protect the union from threats, domestic and foreign. Seizing his opportunity, he quickly developed an array of interconnected policies. Many of these policies were initiated before Congress reconvened in December 1825; most of the rest were proposed in his first annual message.[3]

It was his commitment to the union and to an active federal government that had, in the end, secured Adams's election. With four men dividing the votes (Adams, Clay, Jackson, and William H. Crawford), no candidate had received a majority of either the popular or the electoral vote, though Jackson had received a plurality of each. The final decision passed to the House of Representatives, which had to choose among the top three candidates. Clay, with the fewest electoral votes, lost the chance to become the president himself, but, with his great influence in the House, gained the power to choose between the remaining candidates. Despite his long dispute with Adams over Spanish American policy, the choice seemed clear. Only Adams fully shared Clay's belief that federal energy was needed to cement the bonds between the states and sections of the union. Crawford had actively opposed many of the Monroe administration's efforts to strengthen the nation following the War of 1812, while Jackson had little to recommend him for office except a military reputation—and even that was marked by his fiery temper and his frequent disregard for authority. After "a long conversation" in which Adams "satisf[ied] him with regard to some principles of great public importance," Clay announced his support for Adams. Within weeks, Adams named Clay as his secretary of state. No "bargain" was made, because no bargain was necessary. Clay could not have preferred either of the other candidates; once Clay made clear his stance, Adams could hardly have constructed a cabinet of men who were prominent, represented the major sections of the union, and supported him without including Clay.[4]

In order to strengthen the bonds between the people, states, and sections of the increasingly far-flung union, the new cabinet championed what Adams described as "improvement" and what Clay called the "American System." Each desired an extensive system of roads and canals planned, funded, and managed by the federal government, a protective tariff to support domestic manufactures, a national banking and currency system, and a reasonable federal land policy. Working together, these measures—Adams and Clay calculated—would foster exchange between Americans of different states and sections, balance the often-competing interests of the agricultural, commercial, and manufacturing sectors, insulate American producers and consumers from changes in foreign markets, and promote general prosperity. They would both increase harmony at home and reduce pressures from abroad. They would advance the goals established by the Founders in 1787 and answer the shortcomings exposed by the Embargo and the War of 1812. Adams hoped to go even further. He believed that "no government . . . can accomplish [its] lawful ends . . . but in proportion as it improves the condition of those over whom it is established." As such, he defined "internal improvement" more broadly than most of his contemporaries, including even Clay and the other cabinet members. Adams placed "moral, political, [and] intellectual improvement" alongside material improvements among his goals for the American people and his idea of the duties of the federal government.[5]

Adams inherited from the Founders not only a commitment to union but also an opposition to party. In his view, and theirs, these positions were closely connected. Historically, division into parties or factions had been one of the most common causes of the destruction of republican governments. "Different views of administrative policy," conflicting personal loyalties, and even "dangerous attachments to one foreign nation and antipathies against another" could produce "collisions of party spirit," but such divisions were "in their nature transitory." In a federal republic such as the United States, however, parties might also arise based upon "geographical divisions" that marked "adverse interests of soil, climate, and modes of domestic life." Such parties—Adams, like the Founders, recognized—might be "more permanent, and therefore, perhaps, more dangerous." Sectional parties, more than any others, "threaten[ed] the dissolution of the Union, and with it the overthrow of all the enjoyments of our present lot and all our earthly hopes for the future." Given these concerns, Adams hoped and worked for an end to domestic divisions, both the old ones between Federalists and Republicans and the new ones between the supporters of the rival candidates in the recent presidential election. Believing that most of the people, and even most of the politicians, shared his opposition to parties, Adams expected all Americans to unite behind him.[6]

Most of Adams's specific domestic policies had to await the meeting of Congress in December 1825. But his earliest efforts to promote union and obliterate party appeared in the weeks between his election by the House and his inauguration. He saw his selection of cabinet nominees as an important way to advance his goals. To maintain continuity with his predecessor, he continued in office Attorney General William Wirt and Secretary of the Navy Samuel L. Southard. To balance sectional interests, he chose representatives from each region. To ameliorate factional divisions, he tried to bring each of his defeated rivals into the administration. Adams invited Crawford to remain in the Treasury Department, but he declined. And he considered offering Jackson the War Department, but decided against it when he learned that Jackson "would take in ill part the offer." Adams's inaugural address had also provided an early indication of his commitment to using the federal government to strengthen the union and improve the condition of the people. But it was his first annual message nine months later that gave this general statement a specific form. In it, Adams urged Congress to fund roads and canals, reexamine public land policy, revise the patent system, develop uniform bankruptcy laws, and, broadly, promote "agriculture, commerce, and manufactures." He also championed federal sponsorship of universities, exploration, observatories, and other scientific research. In Adams's view, all of these measures fit within the proper duties and the constitutional means of the federal government. Failing or refusing to use its lawful powers "for the benefit of the people themselves," he insisted, "would be treachery to the most sacred of trusts."[7]

If Adams's internal goals and policies showed the imprint of the thinking of the Founders, his international ones embodied the interweaving of old ideas about threats on the nation's periphery with new concerns about developments throughout the hemisphere. The interest in territorial expansion and the anxiety about immediate neighbors that had lain dormant throughout Adams's second term as secretary of state reemerged during his presidency. Fueled, at least in part, by Clay's understanding of western fears, the new administration turned its attention to the southwest, where the Louisiana-Texas border, in Clay's view, "approache[d] our great western Mart [New Orleans], nearer than could be wished." Such an awareness that foreign interference with the commerce of the Mississippi River could threaten the union between East and West dated to the 1780s and had influenced American policy on the Gulf Coast for decades. Even as it helped to create renewed interest in Texas during Adams's presidency, it also fueled a deepening concern with the status of Spanish Cuba, which could control all of the trade through the Gulf by virtue of its location. Having lost its mainland colonies, Spain seemed destined to lose Cuba, and Puerto Rico, as well. In no one else hands, however, would Cuba be so innocuous. A stronger power, such as France or Great Britain, would surely use it to harass American trade; a weaker one, including an independent Cuba, would surely fall to the British. Even as these concerns focused attention on neighboring Texas and Cuba, increased congressional interest and the approaching expiration of the Convention of 1818 eventually made Oregon and the northwestern boundary an issue once again.[8]

Even though the revival of boundary questions over Texas and Oregon reinvigorated some of the key issues of Adams's first term as secretary of state, most of the problems that preoccupied the new administration involved the major concerns of his second term. Commercial matters continued to receive high priority. Adams remained committed to a set of commercial principles and policies that he insisted the United States had always supported and that he described as "of the most liberal character." "Liberal" commerce encompassed open access to all markets, including colonial ones, full reciprocity of fees and duties for the ships of one nation in the ports of another, and a broad view of neutral rights—including "free ships make free goods," a strict definition of blockades, and a restricted list of contraband. When Adams entered office, he expected to resume negotiations toward a solution to the continuing Anglo-American dispute over access to the British West Indies. He also hoped to conclude new commercial treaties founded upon these principles with European and, perhaps more significant, Spanish American nations. International support for such principles, Adams believed, would benefit all nations by promoting prosperity and reducing conflict. But it would favor the United States perhaps most of all because of the advantages enjoyed by its merchants. Since Congress had endorsed the cornerstone of liberal commerce—the principle of reciprocity—in a January 1824 law, the full weight of the government seemed to support it, holding out the promise of successful negotiations.[9]

The Adams administration also maintained its predecessor's interest in, and approach to, developments to the south. Even though the rebellious colonies had overthrown Spanish authority on the mainland and even though the United States and, in early 1825, Great Britain had recognized their independence, Spain had not accepted its loss. The formal state of war persisted, though almost all of the fighting had ended. Adams remained committed to

a policy of neutrality in the war between Spain and its former colonies. But he still believed that it was the emergence of an independent New World, not the persistence of the formal state of war,
that presented the great challenge to American policymakers. Such
thinking had led to the diplomatic recognition of the former Spanish colonies in early 1822 and to the Monroe Doctrine in late 1823.
It also led Adams and Clay to search for additional ways to promote the goals of diplomatic isolation, republican government, and
liberal commerce among the new nations of Central and South
America. Only a general acceptance of these principles, in their
view, could ensure the security, prosperity, and happiness of the
new states and the American union. In general, however, little
progress had been made toward spreading these principles among
the new states in the three years between American recognition and
Adams's inauguration. The danger of European interference,
whether by invitation or by force, had dissipated, but military leaders, rather than elected officials, frequently held power. At the same
time, as Adams explained to Congress, the new states' continuing
reliance upon "discriminations of commercial favor to other nations, licentious privateers, and paper blockades" marked the limits of their commitment to liberal commerce.[10]

Almost immediately upon entering office, Adams and Clay set
in motion negotiations with a number of nations that they hoped
would help to secure their many and varied goals. In his first two
weeks as secretary of state, Clay prepared instructions for Minister
to Mexico Joel R. Poinsett that directed him to open negotiations
over Texas and the southwestern boundary. A new boundary at the
Rio Brazos, the Colorado River, or the Rio Grande, Clay argued,
would help to prevent future "collissions and misunderstandings"
between the two nations. Over the next few weeks, moreover, Clay
drafted instructions for many of his diplomats abroad that looked
to the conclusion of treaties that placed trade "permanently . . .
upon a footing of fair and perfect reciprocity." Mexico, Buenos Aires,
Brazil, the Central American federation, and Sweden were all to be
invited to adopt reciprocity either by signing a convention or by
unilaterally enacting the regulations necessary to activate the January 1824 law—a step that had already been taken by a long list of
small European nations. In other cases, new commercial negotiations were sought to provide access to colonial markets. Of particular importance to Adams and Clay was the renewal of talks with
Great Britain over the West Indies. Through private and official letters and personal meetings, Adams and Clay impressed upon Rufus

King, the minister to Great Britain, the importance of this issue to them and their willingness to compromise.[11]

As they prepared for a variety of bilateral negotiations on territorial and commercial issues, Adams and Clay also turned to multilateral diplomacy to advance their international goals. In the spring of 1825, they launched what might be described as a "peace initiative" in order to end the war between Spain and its former colonies. The stability that would accompany peace, they calculated, would serve two of their goals. First, it would help to solve the growing problem of Cuba. Ending the war would eliminate the danger of a Colombian or Mexican invasion and ease the pressures for Cuban independence, securing the island for Spain and removing the danger from Great Britain. Second, it would encourage the adoption of American diplomatic, political, and commercial principles by the new states. Peace would free them from making further preparations against Spanish attacks, offering special commercial privileges to Spain or other European powers in exchange for recognition, and continuing their war upon Spanish shipping. They would be able to transfer their governments from military to civilian rule, cease their negotiations with European powers, and curtail their blockades and privateering. By the end of May, the ministers to Mexico, Colombia, Spain, Russia, France, and Great Britain had been sent new instructions explaining their roles in this peace initiative; Adams and Clay had also discussed it with the Mexican, Colombian, Russian, and British ministers in Washington. Mexico and Colombia had already agreed to suspend their planned invasion of Cuba, providing Adams and Clay with a carrot that their minister in Spain and any supporters in Europe could use to entice Spain to end the war.

The administration's other effort at multilateral diplomacy was even more ambitious. In late April 1825, Clay received an invitation to the congress of American nations that had been called by Colombia's Simón Bolívar to convene in Panama. Adams and Clay quickly accepted the invitation. They saw the Panama Congress as a perhaps unique opportunity to spread the American diplomatic, political, and commercial model throughout the New World. The Congress could discuss means for limiting European interference in the hemisphere and agree upon reciprocity as the basis for commerce. Without compromising its neutrality, the United States could use its influence with the new states to check any plans for an invasion of Cuba or Puerto Rico. Adams also viewed the possibility of "establish[ing] American principles of maritime, belligerent, and neutral law" as an "interest of infinite magnitude" for the United States. At Panama, as Clay later noted in his instructions for the mission, treaties "laying the foundations of lasting amity and good neighbourhood," which "would require many years to consummate" in bilateral negotiations, could be settled in "a few months." In Clay's thinking, the mission to the Panama Congress was "the most important ever sent from this Country," excepting only the ones that had negotiated the Treaty of Paris in 1783 and the Treaty of Ghent in 1814.[12]

By the time that the first congressional session of Adams's presidency began in early December 1825, the new administration had already charted an ambitious program for the nation's future. Adams's first annual message to Congress, which he submitted only after lengthy discussions with his cabinet, advanced these goals and policies in three ways. Its most controversial section explained his general views of the purposes, duties, and powers of the federal government, calling for "the internal improvement of our country . . . in a more enlarged extent." The message also detailed the administration's actions during the preceding nine months. Adams announced, for example, that "the invitation [to the Panama Congress had] been accepted" and that ministers had been selected to participate in the Congress "so far as may be compatible with [American] neutrality." Similarly, he noted the initiation or continuation of negotiations on various commercial matters with European and Spanish American nations. The final function of Adams's message was to direct Congress to the specific areas in which it could support the administration's particular initiatives or advance the president's broader goals. With this ambitious program laid out and, wherever possible, set in motion, Adams "await[ed] with cheering hope and faithful cooperation the result of [Congress's] deliberations."[13]

~

If the first nine months of Adams's presidency were marked by great promise and energetic action, the remainder was marred by bitter disappointment and uncharacteristic resignation. Adams and Clay could point to some successes, both at home and abroad. But even these represented only an imperfect or limited version of their expectations. For Adams, the explanation of this failure could be easily traced to the actions of his domestic opponents—the Democratic party that was nominally headed by Jackson, but was actually managed by Vice President Calhoun and New York Senator Martin Van Buren. Adams saw himself and his measures as the victims of "a combination of parties and of public men . . . such as [he] believe[d] never before was exhibited against any man since this Union existed." But party divisions alone cannot explain Adams's failures. As had been the case in the past, his subordinates in the field, at times, created difficulties of their own for the administration. Furthermore, foreign powers—both European and Spanish American—refused to act in the ways expected or desired by Adams and Clay, interposing insurmountable obstacles to some of their policies. Adams deserves some of the blame as well; he responded to the intensifying domestic opposition with political fatalism and physical depression. Even his initial policies need to be examined critically, moreover. Four decades of developments at home and abroad had changed the conditions that had shaped the thinking of the Founders. As president, Adams had to confront the ambiguities and limits of the Founders' commitment to policymaking for the union.[14]

Not all was failure certainly. Some aspects of the American System were advanced during Adams's presidency. His own sweeping vision of "internal improvement" won few converts. Between 1825 and 1829, Congress never even discussed, except mockingly, a national university, scientific expeditions, or the astronomical observatories that the president had unfortunately described as "light-houses of the skies." But the more limited definition of internal improvements as roads and canals met with considerable support. In the four years of Adams's presidency, the federal government spent more than twice as much on roads and canals as under all of his predecessors combined. And, in 1828, Congress passed a tariff that raised the duties on a variety of goods to protective levels. Still, even these successes fell short of Adams's expectations. Congress agreed to fund roads and canals, but abandoned the idea that they would be parts of a system that was planned and managed by the federal government. Instead, the federal government simply bought stock in private companies based upon decisions that served state, local, or party interests more than national ones. In the same way, the Tariff of 1828 emerged from an interplay of political and sectional motives, not from a careful weighing and balancing of the needs of manufacturers, farmers, and merchants. While he signed it into law, Adams admitted that "it was certainly not what I should have thought the best measure for [manufacturers]."[15]

Similarly, Adams and Clay could claim some successes abroad. "Many treaties, founded upon the most liberal and enlightened principles of friendship, commerce and navigation," Clay reminded one group of supporters shortly after he left office, "have been formed." In fact, more treaties were concluded "at the seat of the federal government" during Adams's presidency than "during the thirty-six previous years of the existence of our present constitution." In an 1836 letter, Clay singled out the December 1825 treaty with the Central American federation as the most important of these. It established a perfect reciprocity of trade in all products for the ships of each nation in the ports of the other, "without regard to the place of [the products'] *origin*." It was subsequently used as "a model treaty" because it provided, as Clay explained, for "the most perfect freedom of navigation" that "we can conceive of." But the model was, at best, imperfectly duplicated in other treaties. Clay's later instructions permitted the signing of treaties based upon most-favored-nation status if perfect reciprocity was not attainable. A commercial convention with Mexico was signed in July 1826 on this more limited basis, but was rejected for other reasons. A later treaty with Brazil did not establish even most-favored-nation status, as it allowed Brazil to grant special privileges to Portugal. And a convention with Sweden included a similar exception from most-favored-nation status for the other Baltic nations. In the end, even the "model" treaty with the Central American federation was a disappointment. In 1826, the federation began to dissolve; two years later, it had collapsed entirely, with its member states absorbed by their neighbors.[16]

Balanced against this short list of often mixed successes was a much longer list of often total failures. The attempt to acquire Texas from Mexico, the efforts to reopen the British West Indies to American ships, the peace initiative to end the war between Spain and its former colonies, and the Panama Congress all came to nothing during Adams's presidency. Various factors contributed to these failures. For one thing, President Adams often experienced the same frustrations that Secretary of State Adams had when it came to working through distant subordinates. His representatives to the new Central and South American nations proved especially troublesome. Several never even made it to their posts—some because they died on the way or on arrival—with the result that the United States was left unrepresented for years at a time. In Mexico City, Poinsett ran afoul of his hosts by meddling in Mexican politics, thereby seriously damaging his efforts to secure the acquisition of Texas and a convention on commerce. In Rio de Janeiro, Condy Raguet became so heated in his protests against Brazilian blockades and ship seizures that, without awaiting new instructions, he threatened war, demanded his passport, and returned to the United States. As secretary of state, Adams had often complained of Monroe's failure to control or, at least, recall disobedient agents. As president, Adams acted much as his predecessor had. When Clay strongly urged him to replace Poinsett with "some more suitable person," Adams refused on the grounds that it would appear to "censure" him.[17]

The problems created by the administration's representatives abroad paled before the difficulties created by the nations with whom it negotiated. The United States failed to acquire Texas in this period less because of Poinsett's misbehavior than because of Mexico's unwillingess to cede the potentially valuable region. The administration failed to reopen the trade with the British West Indies primarily due to Great Britain's refusal even to discuss the matter after early 1826. And Adams and Clay failed to arrange an end of the war between Spain and its former colonies largely because of the Spanish "King's unalterable resolution never to abandon his rights" to his empire. Adams's critics, at the time and since, argued that more capable diplomacy on the administration's part would have produced better results. But Mexico, Great Britain, and Spain each had interests that it wanted to protect. And it is in the very nature of diplomacy, of course, that one party alone can prevent an agreement. Adams and Clay certainly missed an early opportunity to reopen talks with Great Britain—in part because they did not understand a law that Parliament enacted in the summer of 1825 and in part because King had not yet reached London. But it remains difficult to identify any step that would have been considered reasonable by either the administration or its critics that would have brought Mexico to cede Texas or Spain to recognize its former colonies at that time.[18]

Domestic—rather than foreign—opposition accounted for much of the administration's failure, though certainly not as much as Adams and Clay thought. The actions of the Democrats struck them so forcefully in part because they were so unexpected. Despite the intensity of the factional divisions that marked the election of 1824 and the charges of a "corrupt bargain" that shrouded its results, Adams and Clay expected all of the fragments of the old Republican party to reunite behind the administration. Evidence that a new "era of good feelings" would not follow Adams's election was certainly available from the start. Even before his inauguration, Adams heard enough rumors and warnings to conclude that the goal of Calhoun's "system of opposition" would be "to bring in General Jackson as the next President." "To this end," Adams noted, "the Administration must be rendered unpopular and odious, whatever its acts and measures may be." During the nine-month congressional recess, however, Adams and Clay increasingly discounted the danger of significant political opposition. They doubted that the friends of Jackson, Calhoun, and Crawford would ever find enough common ground to join forces since, as Clay put it, they did not "[possess] any principle of cohesion." By mid-December 1825, Clay believed that the administration had "gained much strength, in the recess of Congress, [and would] possess all the power and influence which the Executive ought to enjoy." But the discordant elements of the opposition had already begun to coalesce.[19]

Over the next two years, Calhoun and Van Buren assembled a new political party by merging the popular support for Jackson, which lacked clear principles, with the political principles of states' rights and strict construction, which lacked widespread support. The supporters of Jackson, Crawford, and Calhoun came together around the charge that a corrupt bargain had thwarted the public's preference for Jackson and against the principles, proposals, and language of Adams's first annual message. They understood, much better than Adams and Clay, that the concerns of the Founders no longer seemed relevant to most Americans. In his message, Adams called upon Congress and the public to sacrifice the particular interests of localities, sections, and economic sectors to benefit the general interest in union. With so many Americans confident of the durability of the union (despite the slavery issue), the Democrats could easily situate themselves as the defenders of these particular interests against a dangerously intrusive federal government. As Calhoun soon realized, Adams's first annual message—by recommending not just "the measures now required . . . , but all those which may hereafter be required"—cemented the opposition to the administration. It alienated some of the post-War of 1812 supporters of energetic policies who feared that Adams's "injudicious course" would produce a backlash that would "endanger all that [had] been done." And it ensured the hostility of "the friends of State rights" who "[saw] in it a fulfilment of the evils which they [had] anticipated." In the hands of his opponents, Adams recognized too late, the message could be used to "[produce] a crisis involving the liberty and happiness of all future ages."[20]

The opposition undermined or thwarted the administration's efforts in a number of areas. To Adams's surprise, the mission to the Panama Congress served as the "first trial of strength" for the unlikely coalition. Antiadministration forces first tried to block the nominations of Richard C. Anderson and John Sergeant in the Senate and later attempted to defeat the necessary appropriations in the House. While a majority of each house ultimately backed the administration on these questions, the opposition managed to prolong the debates for so long—and thus to delay the departure of Anderson and Sergeant for so long—that neither minister could reach Panama before the Congress adjourned in mid-July without having accomplished anything. Early in the next congressional session, Calhoun predicted that "the great topick of the session [would] be the W[est] India trade." Even as the administration struggled against Great Britain's refusal to negotiate on this issue, the opposition defeated its efforts to apply pressure to the British economy as a way to force a resolution. When the Democrats' substitute measures failed to achieve the desired result, they blamed Adams and Clay. Adams published an anonymous article in the *American Quarterly* defending the American position, in general, and his policy, in particular. But the suspension of all trade between the British West Indies and the United States after the spring of 1827 gave the Democrats one more issue to use against Adams in the election of 1828. As the antiadministration forces gained strength and unity, more and more of Adams's proposals, domestic and foreign, fell before them.[21]

Surprisingly, Adams—whom Ralph Waldo Emerson later aptly described as a "bruiser" who "loves the melee"—responded to this domestic opposition with a degree of fatalism and resignation that doomed both his reelection hopes and his policies. His diary provides ample evidence of a deepening mental and physical depression that was exacerbated by the death of his father on the Fourth of July 1826 and the failure of his three sons to meet his expectations. In the fall of 1826, he wrapped up his father's estate already believing that he would need "a place of retirement from March, 1829, for the remainder of [his] days." The following summer, he confessed in his diary to having had, for several months past, "a sluggish carelessness of life [and] an imaginary wish that it were terminated." He grew inattentive to important affairs and incapable of writing, though he continued to fill pages in his diary. "The most alarming symptom" of his depression, in his own view, was "an aversion to labor" that was "the reverse of that devotion to it which

[had] hitherto sustained [him] in all [his] trials." Instead of battling his opponents, he wasted time at a variety of distractions. He swam (nude) in the Potomac River on most summer days, rode or walked for miles through the still-unfinished capital city, and played billiards in the evenings. Adams also devoted more and more time and energy to the gardens and grounds of the executive mansion, learning the names of the plants, collecting seeds, and planning the beds. After fifty years of "heedlessness" to the natural world around him, Adams—in the midst of a battle for his political future—became utterly engrossed in gardening as a rare form of solace.[22]

What Adams never seems to have realized was that his goals and policies created problems of their own. In trying to apply the thinking of the Founders to the conditions of the 1820s, he discovered its complexity and limits. At home, for example, his failure to see that most Americans and most congressmen no longer believed in sacrificing for the union led him to accept a process for federal policymaking that ultimately threatened his goals. He relied upon Congress to balance the divergent—and, at times, conflicting—interests of localities, states, and sections when it came to internal improvements. By doing so, he effectively abandoned the responsibility for establishing a national system to congressmen who prized local over national interests and who opposed enlarging federal powers. Even as individual road and canal projects received federal funds, there was no effort to coordinate these projects or to bring them under federal control as Adams had intended. In the same way, Adams argued that tariff revisions were "peculiarly the province of the Legislature" since they required a "conciliation" of the different interests of the agricultural, commercial, and manufacturing sectors. Instead of producing a careful balance of interests, however, this approach unleashed a process of logrolling in Congress. The Tariff of 1828—or "Tariff of Abominations," as it was soon known—failed to satisfy any interest. More important, it exacerbated sectional tensions, sparking "threats of disunion" in some southern states that endangered Adams's most fundamental goal.[23]

Abroad, Adams and Clay similarly undermined their most basic goals as they confronted the ambiguities of the thinking of the Founders. Since the 1780s, American policymakers had worried that a powerful neighbor could exert pressures that would tear apart the weak union. Applying this thinking, Adams and Clay looked for ways to acquire Texas from Mexico and secure Cuba for Spain. Mexican and Spanish opposition explained much of the failure of these efforts. But the efforts themselves had harmful consequences. In trying to promote American interests as defined in the 1780s, Adams and Clay ignored the redefinition of American interests that had occurred in the early 1820s with the emergence of an independent New World. Their pressures to acquire Texas, for example, suggested to Mexico that the United States needed to be viewed as "bad neighbors." What Adams and Clay wanted with this most important of the Spanish American states was, of course, the exact opposite—"an intercourse of Amity" and good neighborhood. In the same way, their effort to end the state of war between Spain and its former colonies also proved self-defeating. Their willingness to leave Cuba in Spanish hands produced a backlash against the United States throughout Spanish America, especially in Mexico. More important, by asking Great Britain, France, and Russia to intercede with Spain, Adams and Clay invited European interference in the Western Hemisphere. In a meeting with the Russian minister in May 1825, Adams argued precisely what the Monroe Doctrine had so forcefully denied just eighteen months earlier—that the situation in the New World might be such as to involve "the interests of all the European and all the American powers."[24]

If Adams and Clay showed a continued adherence to the logic of the Founders, despite changed conditions, in their approach to Texas and Cuba, they made a radical break with this thinking in their approach to the New World as a whole. Confronted with the prospect of a multitude of independent sovereignties in eastern North America, the Founders had decided that only a union of all of the American states could secure independence and republican government for each. In the mid-1820s, Americans faced the same prospect on a larger scale. Adams understood the challenge as clearly as anyone. Defending the Panama mission to Congress, he argued that the rise of "eight sovereign and independent nations in our own quarter of the globe [had] placed the United States in a situation not less novel and scarcely less interesting than that in which they had found themselves by their own transition from a cluster of colonies to a nation of sovereign States." The Spanish American revolutions were nearly as significant *for the people of the United States* as their own revolution. In books and pamphlets, newspaper and magazine articles, North and South American authors responded to this development by calling for a hemispheric union that was capable "of securing peace and power *abroad*, peace and happiness at home." But Adams and Clay opposed the extension of the thinking of the Founders in this manner. As Clay flatly explained in the instructions for the Panama mission, "all notion is rejected of an Amphyctionic Council, invested with power finally, to decide controversies between the American States, or to regulate, in any respect, their conduct." Even as they hoped to promote independence and republicanism throughout the New World, Adams and Clay rejected the kind of union that the Founders had viewed as the only way to achieve this goal.[25]

By the end of Adams's presidency, then, little remained of the logic of the Founders that had shaped American policymaking, at home and abroad, for four decades. Adams and Clay certainly still worried that a weak union would dissolve unless federal policymakers devised and implemented energetic measures to keep it together. But the success of their opponents in the midterm congressional elections of 1826 and in the presidential election of 1828 demonstrated that most Americans no longer shared their concerns. More and more congressmen—and there were more and more of them as the population and the number of states grew—viewed their primary responsibility as protecting and promoting their constituents' particular interests in the route of a road or canal or the specifics of a tariff schedule rather than what then-Senator Adams had once described as their "paramount interest in *Union*." At the same time, however, Adams and Clay abandoned the Founders' distinctly American contribution to thinking about international relations. They placed limits on the solution of union by insisting that, while it might preserve the peace and security of an entire continent, it could not work for an entire hemisphere. Approaching their new situation just as any European statesman would have, they decided that, if the United States had to share the New World with other sovereign nations, it had to be the most powerful. As such, they worked against any effort to form a union of all of the Spanish American states that might be larger and stronger than their own union. Promoting peace and amity remained important, but, as Adams admitted in the summer of 1827, the prospect that the relations between the new states and the United States would ever be very close "must be doubtful to those who look forward to human motives."[26]

~

When Adams left office in March 1829, he clearly recognized that the previous four years had brought the defeat of his entire approach to policymaking, not just of his specific policies. He saw this defeat as almost unbounded in its scope. "I fell," he wrote after nearly eight years under President Jackson, "and with me fell, I fear never to rise again, certainly never to rise again in my day, the system of internal improvement by National means and National energies." In this assessment, he was largely correct. He viewed the source of this defeat as obvious. A political party had arisen to oppose him, he noted in his final week in office, precisely because of "the devotion of my life and of all the faculties of my soul to the Union, and to the improvement, physical, moral, and intellectual, of my country." In identifying the Democrats as the source of almost all of his failures, Adams ignored a number of other significant factors. Some of his policies suffered because of the actions of his own subordinates; some failed almost wholly due to the opposition of the foreign powers that Adams relied upon for concessions. But some of his policies undermined their own goals because Adams and his cabinet remained committed to a way of thinking that could not easily be accommodated to conditions that had changed dramatically in four decades. Though his presidency had forced him to confront the complexity and the limits of the Founders' thinking, however, Adams left office committed to it. "The cause of Union and of improvement will remain," he recorded in his diary at the end of February 1829, "and I have duties to it and to my country yet to discharge."[27]

Notes

1. Walter LaFeber, *The American Age: United States Foreign Policy at Home and Abroad since 1750* (New York, 1989), 87; Henry Clay, "Speech at Frederick, Md.," March 18, 1829, *The Papers of Henry Clay*, ed. James F. Hopkins et al., 10 vols. and Supplement (Lexington, Ky., 1959–1992), 8:12 (hereafter *Papers of Clay*); John Quincy Adams (hereafter JQA), diary entry, December 5, 1828, *Memoirs of John Quincy Adams: Comprising Portions of His Diary from 1795 to 1848*, ed. Charles Francis Adams, 12 vols. (Philadelphia, 1874–1877), 8:79 (hereafter *Memoirs*). In a 1982 survey, Adams ranked sixteenth of thirty-six presidents, which placed him in the "above average" category. Still, he trailed each of his five predecessors, as well as Jackson. Twenty years earlier, he had ranked thirteenth of thirty-one (placing him in the "average" category), with only James Monroe of the first seven presidents behind him. See Robert K. Murray and Tim H. Blessing, "The Presidential Performance Study: A Progress Report," *Journal of American History* 70 (December 1983): 535–55.

2. JQA, "Inaugural Address," March 4, 1825, *A Compilation of the Messages and Papers of the Presidents, 1789–1897*, comp. James D. Richardson, 10 vols. (Washington, D.C., 1897–1899), 2:299 (hereafter *Messages of the Presidents*).

3. JQA to John Adams, February 9, 1825, *Memoirs*, 6:504; JQA, "Inaugural Address," March 4, 1825, *Messages of the Presidents*, 2:294.

4. JQA, diary entry, January 9, 1825, *Memoirs*, 6:464, 465.

5. JQA, "First Annual Message," December 6, 1825, *Messages of the Presidents*, 2:311.

6. JQA, "Inaugural Address," March 4, 1825, ibid., 297, 296, 297, 295.

7. JQA, diary entry, February 16, 1825, *Memoirs*, 6:510; JQA, "First Annual Message," December 6, 1825, *Messages of the Presidents*, 2:316.

8. Henry Clay to Joel R. Poinsett, March 26, 1825, *Papers of Clay*, 4:173.

9. JQA, "First Annual Message," December 6, 1825, *Messages of the Presidents*, 2:300.

10. JQA, "Special Message," March 15, 1826, ibid., 333.

11. Henry Clay to Joel R. Poinsett, March 26, 1825, *Papers of Clay*, 4:173; Henry Clay to William C. Somerville, April 14, 1825, ibid., 256.

12. JQA, diary entry, April 23, 1825, *Memoirs*, 6:531; Henry Clay to Richard C. Anderson Jr. and John Sergeant, May 8, 1826, *Papers of Clay*, 5:315; Henry Clay to Albert Gallatin, November 11, 1825, ibid., 4:814.

13. JQA, "First Annual Message," December 6, 1825, *Messages of the Presidents*, 2:311, 302, 317.

14. JQA, diary entry, "Day" [February 1829], *Memoirs*, 8:100.

15. JQA, "First Annual Message," December 6, 1825, *Messages of the Presidents*, 2:313; JQA to James H. McCulloh, October 1, 1828, Adams Papers, Massachusetts Historical Society, Boston (microfilm), reel 148 (hereafter Adams Papers).

16. Henry Clay, "Speech at Frederick, Md.," March 18, 1829, *Papers of Clay*, 8:12; Henry Clay to Robert Walsh Jr., April 25, 1836, ibid., 845; Henry Clay to William Tudor, March 29, 1828, ibid., 7:201.

17. Henry Clay to JQA, August 23, 1827, ibid., 6:951; JQA to Henry Clay, August 31, 1827, ibid., 985.

18. Alexander H. Everett to Henry Clay, October 20, 1825, *Diplomatic Correspondence of the United States Concerning the Independence of the Latin-American Nations*, ed. William R. Manning, 3 vols. (Washington, D.C., 1925), 3:2068.

19. JQA, diary entry, February 11, 1825, *Memoirs*, 6:507; Henry Clay to James Brown, December 12, 1825, *Papers of Clay*, 4:895, 896.

20. John C. Calhoun to [Samuel L. Gouverneur ?], December 18, 1825, *Papers of John C. Calhoun*, ed. Robert L. Meriwether et al., 24 vols. to date (Columbia, S.C., 1959–), 10:58 (hereafter *Papers of Calhoun*); JQA, diary entry, January 12, 1826, *Memoirs*, 7:104.

21. JQA to Levi Lincoln, April 7, 1826, Adams Papers, reel 148; John C. Calhoun to James E. Colhoun, December 24, 1826, *Papers of Calhoun*, 10:240.

22. Ralph Waldo Emerson, journal entry, February 8, 1843, quoted in William Lee Miller, *Arguing About Slavery: John Quincy Adams and the Great Battle in the United States Congress* (New York, 1996), 297; JQA, diary entry, "Day" [September 1826], *Memoirs*, 7:149; JQA, diary entry, "Day" [July 1827], ibid., 311; JQA, diary entry, October 17, 1827, ibid., 339; JQA, diary entry, April 9, 1827, ibid., 255.

23. JQA to James H. McCulloh, October 1, 1828, Adams Papers, reel 148; JQA, diary entry, December 31, 1828, *Memoirs*, 8:88.

24. Henry G. Ward to Charles Vaughan, May 23, 1826, John A. Doyle, ed., "The Papers of Sir Charles Vaughan," *American Historical Review* 7

(January 1902): 323; Henry Clay to Joel R. Poinsett, March 26, 1825, *Papers of Clay*, 4:167; JQA, diary entry, May 19, 1825, *Memoirs*, 7:10.

25. JQA, "Special Message," March 15, 1826, *Messages of the Presidents*, 2:330; "Mutius Scævola," *Daily National Intelligencer*, April 26, 1825; Henry Clay to Richard C. Anderson Jr. and John Sergeant, May 8, 1826, *Papers of Clay*, 5:314.

26. JQA, [notes for speech on] "Proposed Amendment to the Constitution on Representation," [December 1804], *Writings of John Quincy Adams*, ed. Worthington Chauncey Ford, 7 vols. (New York, 1913–1917), 3:88; JQA to Richard Rush, August 16, 1827, Adams Papers, reel 149.

27. JQA to Charles W. Upham, February 2, 1837, Edward H. Tatum Jr., ed., "Ten Unpublished Letters of John Quincy Adams, 1796–1837," *Huntington Library Quarterly* 4 (April 1941): 383; JQA, diary entry, "Day" [February 1829], *Memoirs*, 8:100, 101.

6

An Unexpected Career

1829–1848

Few American presidents have done as much with their lives after leaving the White House, or the President's Mansion as it was still known in 1829, as John Quincy Adams. None of Adams's predecessors, and few of his successors, remained deeply involved in political activity at either the state or national level. In the first weeks after his overwhelming loss to Andrew Jackson in the election of 1828, Adams gave every indication that he too would retire from political life. He admitted "that it would be impossible . . . to divest [himself] of a deep interest in whatever should affect the welfare of the country." But "after the 3d of March [1829]," he informed Henry Clay, "I should consider my public life as closed, and take from that time as little part in public concerns as possible." After just two years, however, Adams entered upon a "second career" as a member of the House of Representatives. From the meeting of the Twenty-second Congress in December 1831 until his death in February 1848, the former president represented his home district in Washington. As a congressman during these "retirement" years, Adams won greater fame, earned more respect, and incurred deeper hatred than at any point during his first career as a diplomat, cabinet member, and president. Northerners, particularly antislavery Northerners, increasingly celebrated him as a defender of their basic rights and of cherished American values, while Southerners, particularly slaveholding Southerners, increasingly attacked him as a threat to their way of life and to the union.[1]

During this second career, Adams gradually developed a new way of thinking about "the welfare of the country." His election as a congressman represented something of a liberation for Adams, both from his lifelong efforts to fulfill the expectations of his parents and from his constant striving to behave as a "man of the whole union." As a member of the House of Representatives, Adams had a duty to act in behalf of the interests and concerns of his constituents. He also had more freedom to act according to the dictates of his own conscience. Still, even as a "man of the Plymouth District of the Commonwealth of Massachusetts," Adams remained committed to an energetic government and a permanent union. And he continued to display an interest in, and mastery of, foreign relations. Increasingly, however, he believed that the federal government had fallen into the hands of men who would use its power not for the end of improving the condition of all of its citizens, but for the "purpose of enlarging the dominion [of slavery] and rivetting forever the Slave holding domination of the Union." The drive to annex Texas, the willingness to compromise American claims to Oregon, and the machinations to spark a war with Mexico that might lead to further expansion in the Southwest all offered evidence to support this analysis. On a few occasions, and always with great hesitation, in these final years, Adams questioned the value of a union that seemed to protect the great stain upon the nation's principles better than the principles themselves. His increasingly frequent predictions of a dismal future for a union that he still considered essential marked his growing despair about the persistence of slavery and its impact upon American policy.[2]

~

While Adams's decision to enter into a second career in the House of Representatives represented a clear break with the past, his course once in Congress did not. Both the precedents set by his five presidential predecessors and the expectations fixed by his parents called for a nearly complete retirement from public affairs. His father, for example, had closely followed state and national politics during the twenty-five years of his retirement, but had only returned to the public stage on one brief occasion and, even then, in an essentially ceremonial position. At first, Adams expected to follow this example by leaving future problems to the next generation of Adamses and confining his labors to the issues of the past. Within just eighteen months of leaving the presidency, he reversed this course by agreeing to be considered a candidate for congressman. In his first years in Congress, Adams showed that his concerns and principles remained consistent with the past, even if his presence in the House was unheard of for a former president. His support for an energetic federal government led him to criticize and challenge the states' rights and strict constructionist views of the Jackson administration. Similarly, his devotion to a permanent union ensured that he would oppose any threat to its stability, whether it came from South Carolinians willing to nullify the tariff or Georgians willing to defy the Supreme Court over Indian policy. As had been the case during his Senate years, moreover, Adams charted a course that was independent of any party, joining with the antiadministration Whigs on most issues, but supporting the Democrats on some critical economic and diplomatic questions.

When Adams left the presidency in March 1829, he clearly intended to retire from public life almost entirely. Like his father before him, Adams expected to pass the responsibility for serving the nation through political activity on to his sons. In the spring of 1827, as it became obvious that he would not be reelected, Adams recorded in his diary: "My own career is closed. My hopes, such as are left me, are centred upon my children." With his three sons carrying the Adams name into the future, he would be free to attend to the Adamses' past. In the final months of his presidency, he had become embroiled in a controversy over his assertion that New England Federalists had plotted to secede from the union on a number of occasions between the Louisiana Purchase and the Hartford Convention. Much of the battle between the president and a group of former Federalists was waged in the nation's newspapers. Adams also compiled a set of documents and wrote a lengthy manuscript in support of his position. During the spring of 1829, he prepared another long manuscript on the history of parties in the United States that blasted both his father's and his own political enemies. His most substantial retirement project as steward of the family's reputation was a biography of John Adams. During the summer of 1829, he began this project by trying to organize his father's papers and starting to read histories of New England, the other American colonies, and Great Britain. By the end of the summer, he even began writing, with the goal of completing one page per day.[3]

These plans quickly collapsed. None of his sons had ever come close to satisfying his expectations or shown any sign that they were likely to do so in the future. The oldest, George Washington, struggled with alcohol, debt, heartbreak, and the pressure to live up to his name. In late April 1829, while traveling to Washington to help with his parents' return to Quincy, he either fell or, more likely, jumped off a steamship and drowned. The second son, John, had evinced no political inclinations, even as his father's private secretary during his presidency, and was barely competent at managing the family's finances. In time, the youngest, Charles Francis, would enter prominently into national affairs; in the spring of 1829, however, he was just twenty-one years old. Deeply affected by George's death, Adams acknowledged that, at least for the present, his sons would not fulfill his hopes for the family's future. At the same time, he began to see his own shortcomings as the steward of the family's past. His first two efforts as a historian—on New England separatism and American political parties—quickly devolved into undisguised attacks on his enemies and blatant justifications of himself and his father; he published neither of them. The biography of his father seemed likely to follow this pattern. Although he believed that "biography may be written perhaps with a more daring hand than general history," he still realized that he would have to weigh what to say about all of the prominent men with whom his father had battled during his life. Adams thought that history should be balanced and impartial; but he could get excited only about issues that touched upon himself or his father and that involved current controversy. Writing about the past interested him only when it served political purposes in the present.[4]

With his initial intentions for his retirement years quickly defeated by his sons' and his own limitations, Adams became very interested when local Republicans approached him in September 1830 about running for Congress. He remained old-fashioned enough in his republicanism that he refused to do anything that, to his mind, looked like running for office or "asking for a vote." Still, he made it clear that he did not consider it inappropriate for a former president to serve in Congress and that he would probably accept the office if "the people [acted] spontaneously" and chose him by a wide margin. His family, particularly his wife and youngest son, strongly opposed the idea, fearing that it would wreck his health, strain their finances, and expose him to new attacks. But Adams warmed to the idea without regard for his family's expectations. When he carried the election by a wide margin, he labored to convince himself (and the succeeding generations of family members that he expected to read his diary) that his victory was "a misfortune" that filled him with "deep concern and anxious forebodings." It would expose him to "political rancor and personal malignity" and place him once more "amidst the breakers of the political ocean." But Adams could not entirely conceal his happiness. He thrilled at having "received nearly three votes in four throughout the district" and admitted: "My election as President of the United States was not half so gratifying to my inmost soul." For sixty years, Adams had worked toward the goals set by his parents in his childhood. He now prepared to embark upon a new career that was entirely his own, contrary to the wishes of his wife and son and the example of his father.[5]

Adams returned to politics committed to principles that had guided him for decades, but that seemed not to carry much weight with the administration, Congress, the states, or the people. He had devoted his presidency to creating "a permanent and regular system" under which the energies of the federal government could be used to improve the lives of its citizens and strengthen the bonds of the union. His efforts had provided a focal point for Democratic unity. When he left office, Adams had predicted that Jackson's presidency would "be the day of small things." From the start, Jackson seemed determined to abandon almost every area of federal activity. As early as May 1830, Adams believed "that the Indians [were] already sacrificed; that the public lands [would] be given away; [and] that domestic industry and internal improvement [would] be strangled." "When the public debt will be paid off and the bank charter expired," he lamented, "there will be no great interest left upon which the action of the General Government will operate." Each of these areas of federal action had also served as "ties, to hold the Union together." Over the next few years, the policies of Jackson and his congressional supporters met or exceeded Adams's fears in each of these areas. After battling the administration in the House for three sessions marked by Indian removal, the bank war, and tariff reductions, Adams concluded in July 1834 that "the system of administration for the government of the Union [had been] radically and . . . irretrievably vitiated."[6]

Adams's devotion to a permanent union did not just lead him to criticize the administration's surrender of federal energy to "State rights[,] negro Slavery, and agrarian rapacity." It also ensured that he would fiercely oppose state officials who defied federal authority over such issues as the tariff and the Indians. The South Carolina nullifiers and their leader, John C. Calhoun, came under special attack for their argument that any state could "nullify" within its own borders a federal law that it considered unconstitutional until three-fourths of the states upheld the law through a constitutional amendment. In December 1828, President Adams had included a warning against this doctrine in his annual message to Congress. As the controversy escalated, Congressman Adams seized an opportunity to warn the people about the danger and seriousness of nullification. Asked to give the Fourth of July oration in Quincy, Adams delivered an address that attacked nullification at its base by denying any real sovereignty to the states outside of the union. Nullification in any form, by any number of states, he saw as "neither more nor less than treason, skulking under the shelter of despotism." "The doctrine in all its parts," he wrote in an account of his oration, "is so adverse to my convictions, that I can view it in no other light than as *organized civil War*." Such a strong warning seemed essential to Adams for two reasons. He doubted, incorrectly as it turned out, that Jackson would stand up to the nullifiers after having abandoned federal authority to the states on so many other issues. And he insisted, as he had for years, that the future of the American people depended upon the union. "The preservation of the Union," he noted in another account of his speech, "is to me what the destruction of Carthage was to Cato—the conclusion of every Discourse."[7]

As a senator in the early 1800s, Adams had prided himself on being a "man of the whole country" instead of a "man of a party." As a congressman in the early 1830s, he generally maintained his political independence, but usually acted as the representative of his district no less than as a spokesman of the whole union. When Adams returned to Congress in December 1831, the political system was in such a fluid state that it would have been very difficult for him to have followed a single party. Just as the Democratic party had coalesced during Adams's presidency out of the opposition to his administration, the Whig party was forming out of the opposition to Jackson's administration. But the anti-Jackson elements— which included Clay's National Republicans, predominantly Northern Anti-Masons, and Southern nullifiers—were so diverse that it took years for them to form even an unstable alliance. In this chaotic situation, Adams moved independently. He joined with the National Republicans against the Democrats on most of the issues that he associated with "improvement," including the national bank, protective tariffs, and roads and canals. Adams had long viewed such measures as critical for the union; he also recognized that they would benefit his district, where manufacturing was rapidly overtaking farming as the main economic activity. At the same time, he fought against many National Republicans, as well as the

Democrats, over the political power of the secretive Masonic Order, a controversial subject in the late 1820s and early 1830s that was important to him and to his constituents.[8]

Adams also hesitated to unite with Whig leaders such as Clay and Massachusetts Senator Daniel Webster whenever he thought that they were opposing Jackson for purely political purposes. As a result, Adams found himself supporting the administration on some important issues. In 1832, he worked with Jackson's secretary of the treasury to craft a compromise tariff that dissatisfied Clay. He also broke with Clay by arguing that the president's desire to pay off the national debt in full "ought to be indulged, and not opposed"; unlike Jackson, Adams then expected to devote all of the government's excess revenue to improvement. As had happened with the Louisiana Purchase in 1803 and the Embargo in 1807, moreover, Adams made his independence especially clear in foreign affairs. During Jackson's second term, a dispute with France over damages claimed by American merchants dating back to the Napoleonic era threatened an explosion. As secretary of state and president, Adams had pressed these claims without success. In 1831, Jackson concluded a treaty with France that scheduled payments totalling $5 million. When France failed to pay, Jackson asked Congress to authorize reprisals. Adams privately believed that the president's anger at France had led him to mishandle the affair. Publicly, he sided with Jackson in defiance of Webster and other Whigs. "The principle with which I have gone through life, under every administration of the Government," he noted, "has been, in controversies with foreign powers, to sustain the existing authorities of my own Country, especially and most zealously when the *right* of the main question was on our side, and the *wrong* on the side of the foreigner." Largely as a result of Adams's efforts, the House passed a bill appropriating funds for defense against France that Webster had defeated in the Senate.[9]

Adams's return to public life as a member of the House of Representatives had mixed effects. The depression and fatalism that had marked his presidency and early retirement faded before a renewed excitement about political battles and public affairs. Despite his age and infirmities, he discovered new energy that he poured into his committee assignments, House speeches, public addresses, correspondence, and diary. Just as Louisa Catherine and Charles Francis had predicted, his return to the government exposed him to personal and political attacks. "If I should say there was a combination of all the competitors for the Presidency, and of all their retainers to accomplish my ruin as a Public man, and the ruin of my character as an honest man," he wrote his son in the spring of 1836, "I should not depart unduly from the truth—in my own be- lief not at all." At the same time, the state of national affairs in the first half of the 1830s was a source of deep concern for Adams. In his view, the idea of an energetic federal government committed to improvement had been not only "systematically renounced and denounced" by the Democrats but also "undisguisedly abandoned by H. Clay, ingloriously deserted by J. C. Calhoun, and silently given up by D. Webster." Having long "imagin[ed] that this federative Union was to last for ages," Adams now "disbelieve[d] its dura- tion for twenty years, and doubt[ed] its continuance for five." He foresaw the same consequences from the collapse of the union in 1834 as he had in 1794. Americans would "go the way of all the world, and split up into an uncertain number of rival communi- ties, enemies in war, in peace friends."[10]

~

Beginning in the mid-1830s, Adams's concern for the present, and dread for the future, condition of the union and the people deepened in the context of his increased focus upon slavery. He had thought at great length about the threat that the demarcation between Northern free states and Southern slave states posed to the union during the Missouri Crisis of 1819–1821. At that time, he had seen the crisis as "a mere preamble—a title-page to a great tragic volume"—and accepted the compromise that resolved it. In the early 1830s, antislavery forces became more radical in their de- mands and methods, fueling antiabolitionist sentiment and action throughout the nation and helping to generate new proslavery ar- guments in the South. Adams initially "hope[d] to have no con- cern" with what he described as "the Slave and Abolition whirligig." While he never fully supported the abolitionists, he became increas- ingly convinced that the Democratic administrations of Andrew Jackson and Martin Van Buren were managed upon "*Southern prin- ciples*[—the] whole compass of which revolve[d] upon one central point, the support and perpetuation of the *peculiar institution of the South*." He found clear evidence of this system in the suppression of the right to petition Congress through the "gag rule," the effort to add Texas to the union as one or more slave states, and the tol- eration of the international slave trade apparent in the handling of the famed *Amistad* case. On each of these issues, Adams devoted his mental, oratorical, and parliamentary abilities to thwarting the Southern "slave power" and defending American principles.[11]

At the time of the Missouri Crisis, Adams articulated fairly clearly his thinking about the relationship between slavery, the federal government, and the union in the pages of his diary and in meetings with cabinet members and select Northern congressmen. Slavery was a multifaceted evil that "pervert[ed] human reason," "taint[ed] the very sources of moral principle," and "polluted" Southern and national politics. It existed in some places as a legacy of British, French, or Spanish colonialism. It was protected in those places by the "morally and politically vicious" bargain made at the constitutional convention that reserved "the regulation, exclusion, or abolition of slavery" to the states. "Where slavery does not exist," Adams argued, "neither Congress, nor the State Legislature, nor the people have any rightful power to establish it." Congress's powers over slavery did include banning the interstate slave trade and the importation of slaves into the territories. Even within these limits, Adams saw a number of ways in which the United States could rid itself of this "great and foul stain." Emancipation might occur peacefully through "the gradually bleaching process of intermixture" between white and black or through a new constitutional convention. It seemed more likely to come about violently. A war—whether with a foreign power or between slaves and masters or between North and South—would activate the Constitution's war powers clause, giving Congress the power to abolish slavery. As much as Adams hated the thought of disunion, he was willing to consider it at some future period upon "the question of slavery, and no other," if it would make possible a reorganization of the union "on the fundamental principle of emancipation."[12]

Slavery never completely disappeared from national politics following the Missouri Crisis; but it clearly gained new force during the early 1830s. In pamphlets, speeches, newspapers, and petitions, a new generation of antislavery activists called for the immediate and uncompensated emancipation of all slaves and denounced as impractical and immoral gradual measures such as colonization schemes. Even in the North, these abolitionists often met with opposition, harassment, and violence from men and women of all classes. In the South, the intensification of antislavery activism coincided with one of the most surprising and deadly instances of slave violence, the Nat Turner Rebellion in Virginia in August 1831. With slavery under attack from within and without, Southerners moved quickly to defend it. Southern politicians, essayists, and orators developed a new proslavery argument that tried to show the benefits of their system for whites and blacks. State, county, and city governments acted to close their communities to any form of antislavery thought or action, whether it came from Northerners, slaves, or Southern whites. In Washington, Southerners used their influence in the cabinet and their votes in Congress to support slavery. Jackson closed the mails to abolitionist literature and asked Congress to pass a censorship law sustaining his action. In response to the hundreds of antislavery petitions that reached Congress each session, Southern congressmen, backed by most Northern Democrats, called for a "gag rule." Under this rule, abolitionist or antislavery petitions would be placed on the table and would never be read or discussed. The right to petition Congress survived only in the most technical sense.

Despite his own antislavery sentiments, Adams remained reluctant to join forces with the abolitionists in the early and mid-1830s. Certain that "the slavery question" was "the most dangerous of all the subjects for public contention," he feared its effects upon both the union and himself. In August 1835, he noted that Southerners might "separate from the Union, in terror of the emancipation of their slaves." Aware that the growth and "zeal" of the abolitionists had "kindle[d] the opposition . . . into a flame," Adams worried about getting burned. "My principles and my position," he noted, "make it necessary for me to be more circumspect in my conduct." "The most insignificant error of conduct in me at this time would be my irredeemable ruin in this world." Privately and publicly, Adams disagreed with the abolitionists about the wisdom of many of their proposals, such as abolishing slavery in the District of Columbia and prohibiting the interstate slave trade. Even as he deliberately distanced himself from them, he inadvertently transformed himself into one of their most effective champions. What they requested of Congress may have been of questionable expediency, but their right to request it through petitions was of unquestionable constitutionality. For Adams, the "gag rule" was part of an attack on the most basic rights of Northern citizens— freedom of speech, freedom of the press, and the right of petition. From 1835 until its repeal in 1845, Adams fought against it in any form. In the process, he blasted slaveholders, Southern politicians, and their Northern allies. And he made public his view that, once the "slaveholding States [became] the theatre of war, civil, servile, or foreign, . . . the war powers of Congress [would] extend to interference with the institution of slavery in every way," including emancipation.[13]

If the "gag rule" offered one inducement to draw Adams into a conflict that he had hoped to avoid, the Texas question quickly provided another. As secretary of state, Adams had abandoned the weak American claim to Texas west of the Sabine River to Spain in the Transcontinental Treaty of 1819. As president, he had permitted Secretary of State Clay to negotiate with Mexico for the purchase of Texas in 1825 and 1827. His successor had openly renewed the diplomatic effort to acquire Texas. More important, Jackson— Adams became convinced—had also covertly encouraged the growing population of Americans in Texas to separate from Mexico and request annexation by the United States. These efforts came to fruition in 1836 when the Texans declared their independence, defeated the Mexican army with the aid of volunteers from the Southern states, forced a treaty recognizing their independence from the captured Mexican president, and requested admission into the union. Adams saw a vast difference between his and Jackson's labors to acquire Texas. The most significant difference, in his view, was the matter of slavery. In the negotiation of the Transcontinental Treaty, "the question of Slavery [had] never presented itself at all." By the time that Adams and Clay had attempted to purchase Texas, Mexico had passed a gradual emancipation law ending slavery. "If the cession had then been made," Adams later explained, "it would have been of a Territory purged from that foul infection." In the same year that Jackson initiated his efforts, Mexico ended slavery immediately by decree.[14]

Adams eventually traced "the conspiracy to sever from Mexico the region to the Rio del Norte [Rio Grande] . . . , and to unite it with our Southern States" to Mexico's abolition decree. He included among the conspirators: "the Slave holding emigrants from our Country into Texas, . . . the Politician Planters of our Southern States, [and] the Bank, Land, and Stock jobbers, and Editors of popular newspapers in the North." In Adams's opinion, the immediate goal was to "[wrest] from Mexico territory enough for nine States as large as Kentucky" that would be added to the union with slavery reestablished. But Jackson, Van Buren, and their supporters also seemed willing to go much further. Adams soon decided that the nation was "in the most iminent danger of being involved in [a] conflagration" over Texas which would "be nothing less than a foreign, a civil, a servile and an Indian war combined in one." In this war, he explained in May 1836, "we have been or are to be the aggressors." "A War with Mexico, for the re-establishment of Slavery in . . . Texas, and for the conquest and annexation of Texas, and other portions of Mexico[,] to our Union [as slave states], and the re-subjugation of emancipated slaves, . . . and the extermination of the Indians whom we have been driving like swine into a pen West of the Mississippi"—all seemed to Adams to be "parts of one System of War policy." Even after his early fears failed to materialize and after, first, Jackson and, then, Van Buren rejected Texas's request for annexation, Adams insisted that "the whole South" and the administration wanted not only to annex Texas but also to provoke Mexico into a war that "would be a golden harvest to the South and West."[15]

Throughout the mid-1830s, Adams worked diligently to thwart what he saw as the Jackson and Van Buren administrations' plans for Texas. He credited himself with being the first congressman to expose Jackson's "secret labours," which he hoped would "open the eyes of the People of the North." In early July 1836, he tried to table and, when that failed, voted against a resolution that urged the administration to recognize Texas as an independent nation as soon as it established a de facto government. Adams presented as many petitions against the annexation of Texas as he could and used them, whenever possible, to speak against it. In late December 1837, he defeated what he saw as a Southern plot to use outstanding claims against Mexico as the basis for a war by prodding Van Buren to accept a Mexican offer to arbitrate. For three weeks in the summer of 1838, Adams spoke out for part of each day in a long attack on annexation and slavery. He could have had the floor when Congress reconvened in December, but, by then, Texas had withdrawn its request for annexation. In private letters and public speeches, Adams made clear the reasons for his opposition to annexing slavery. He saw a "great *Constitutional* objection" to the annexation of one independent nation to another "by the mere authority of their ordinary Legislature" rather than by a constitutional convention. "The *insurmountable* objection," however, in Adams's thinking, was "to an union with *reinstituted* Slavery." As he explained to one opponent of annexation, and also admitted in Congress, "there [was] no valid and permanent objection to the acquisition of Texas, but the indelible stain of Slavery." If Texas would once again abolish slavery, Adams was prepared to set aside his constitutional concerns and admit it to the union.[16]

With the Texas issue temporarily quieted by the withdrawal of its annexation request, Adams found himself once again pushed to the margins of an abolitionist movement that he did not fully support; this situation did not last long. Another issue with an international dimension drew him back into antislavery activity. In late August 1839, the *Amistad* was brought into New London, Connecticut. On board were Africans who had been enslaved in Africa, sold in Havana, and loaded onto the *Amistad* for shipment to remote Cuban sugar plantations. Nearly two months earlier, they had seized the ship and tried to return to Africa, but their Cuban "owners" had led them instead toward the United States. Once in New London, the Cubans claimed that the Africans were rebel slaves. The federal district attorney charged them with piracy and murder and threw them into jail, but hoped that the administration could find some way of turning them over to Spain before the court convened. Van Buren shared this wish. After hearing from the Spanish minister, the cabinet decided that the Africans should be viewed as slaves and removed from the courts as soon as possible. A public outcry erupted as abolitionists argued that the *Amistad* Africans were free men and women who had been illegally enslaved. As the case worked its way through the courts, Adams grew more and more interested. He wrote private letters in support of the Africans' cause that made their way into newspapers and lawyers' arguments. But he became openly involved with the case only when the administration appealed to the Supreme Court after losing in both the district and circuit courts. His seven-and-one-half-hour closing argument helped the men and women of the *Amistad* to win their freedom finally.

In the mid- and late-1830s, Adams found clear evidence that the federal government had fallen entirely under the control of Southern slaveholders. Led by Jackson and Van Buren, the Democrats seemed intent upon "sacrific[ing] the rights of Northern freedom to slavery and the South." The "gag rule," the closing of the mails to abolitionist literature, the Texas revolution, and the *Amistad* case provided mounting evidence in support of Adams's analysis. Even on the most significant questions, such as the annexation of Texas, moreover, the North appeared unwilling to check the South's dominance by asserting its own interests and defending its rights. In this context, Adams's predictions for the future of the federal union and its republican principles grew increasingly dark. Stimulated by the success of the Texas revolution and the exposure of

Mexican weakness, the public seemed to want war and empire. "The whole [of Mexico] must be invaded and conquered by our People," he warned in April 1837. "Nor do I see where our encroachments will stop, short of Cape Horn." But, he wondered, "what are to become of our *Liberties*?" Eight months later, he imagined that annexing a slaveholding Texas would be a mere prelude to annexing a slaveholding Cuba. That event seemed likely to prompt Great Britain—the world's antislavery leader—to launch "a War for the express purpose of abolishing Slavery in this Hemisphere. Our Confederation then, if not sooner," Adams calculated, "will fall to pieces."[17]

~

The course of American foreign policy in the final years of Adams's life only intensified these concerns. Any hope that the election of the Whig candidate, William Henry Harrison, in 1840 might bring new policies at home and abroad was dashed by his death a month after his inauguration. Adams described his successor, John Tyler, as "a political sectarian of the slave-driving, Virginian, Jeffersonian school, principled against all improvement, with all the interests and passions and vices of slavery rooted in his moral and political constitution." Under Tyler and his successor, the Democrat James K. Polk, Southern slaveholders, in Adams's assessment, tightened their hold over the federal government. Tyler renewed the effort to annex Texas, which he achieved in his final days in office. As a candidate, Polk also supported annexation; as president, he pressured Mexico to sell additional territory and, ultimately, into a war. At the same time, after asserting the broadest possible claim to Oregon, Polk accepted a compromise treaty that surrendered a vast area for potential free states to Great Britain. Each of these measures—the annexation of Texas, the Mexican War, and the abandonment of Oregon north of the 49th parallel—served to confirm Adams's fear that Northern interests and American principles mattered less to policymakers than Southern slavery. "Our Country if we have a Country is no longer the same," he wrote despairingly to Richard Rush in late 1845. "The polar Star of our Foreign Relations [under President James Monroe] was Justice, it is now Conquest. Their vital Spirit was then Liberty it is now Slavery."[18]

The Texas question had remained relatively dormant for a few years before Tyler revived it in late 1841. Anxious to add Texas to the union, he tried to bluster Mexico into ceding its claim to the province by stirring up a war fever in the United States. At the same time, pro-administration newspapers labored to soothe Northern concerns about the political power that would accrue to the South with the admission of more slave states. Adams spoke out against these efforts in Congress, thwarting Tyler's plans, at least temporarily, in April 1842. A year later, Adams, first, tried to bring to a vote a resolution declaring the annexation of Texas to be unconstitutional and, then, joined with twelve other antislavery congressmen to issue a public letter asserting that annexation would effectively dissolve the union. In early 1844, Tyler submitted a treaty with Texas to the Senate. Secretary of State Calhoun publicly advocated the treaty—which would have admitted Texas into the union as up to five slave states—as critical for the defense of slavery against the threat of British-led abolitionism. Adams worried that it would spark a "great struggle between slavery and freedom throughout the world." When the Senate rejected it in June 1844, he described the outcome "as a deliverance, I trust, by the special interposition of Almighty God, of my country and of human liberty from a conspiracy comparable to that of Lucius Sergius Catilina." "The annexation of Texas," he believed, would have been just "the first step to the conquest of all Mexico, of the West India Islands, of a maritime, colonizing, slave-tainted monarchy, and of extinguished freedom."[19]

As Adams feared, however, the defeat of the treaty proved to have been "a mere temporary deliverance" in the aftermath of the presidential election of 1844. Tyler had failed in his bid to win the nomination of either party. The Whig Clay had pledged not to annex Texas. But the Democrat Polk had run on a platform that called for the "reannexation of Texas." During the campaign, Adams highlighted this issue in a widely reprinted address to the Young Men's Whig Club in Boston. He urged his audience—and by extension all of the North's young men—to "burnish [their] armor" for "the deadly conflict of arms" between "the spirit of freedom and the spirit of slavery" that seemed inevitable upon the annexation of Texas. Polk's victory over Clay, though by a narrow margin, was viewed by both the Democrats and Tyler as a mandate for annexation. In the final months of his presidency, Tyler asked Congress to annex Texas by joint resolution, which would require a simple majority in each house rather than the two-thirds majority that had eluded him in the Senate six months earlier. Adams spoke and voted against the resolution. Still, he quickly perceived that Tyler's subversion of the regular, constitutional process for interacting with foreign nations would succeed. The question of whether Congress had the power to annex Texas in any manner, and especially by joint resolution, would simply be "decided by the will" to do so. "The Constitution is a menstrous rag," Adams wrote in his diary in disgust, "and the Union is sinking into a military monarchy." The passage of the joint resolution consummated "the heaviest calamity that ever befell myself and my country."[20]

Paired with the "reannexation of Texas" in the Democratic platform of 1844 was the "reoccupation of Oregon." Polk and the Democrats campaigned on a promise to end the joint occupation of the region with Great Britain and secure Oregon for the United States not to 49° north latitude (the border with British Canada east of the Rockies), but to 54°40' (the southern limit of Russian Alaska). As secretary of state and president, Adams had offered the British a line at the 49th parallel from the Rockies to the Pacific. But, he later insisted, this offer had been "made under the impression that it would not be accepted." Instead, it was intended "to preserve the peace . . . and postpone the issue of the controversy until the time should come when we should be able to maintain our claims by an appeal, if necessary, to arms." By the mid-1840s, Adams was willing to join with the administration in pressing the American claim to its fullest extent. Even as he argued that the annexation of Texas had involved "the perfidious robbery and dismemberment of Mexico," Adams denied that Great Britain had any legitimate claim to Oregon "whatever." Using the language of Manifest Destiny, he claimed that the United States wanted Oregon "to fulfil the commands of Almighty God to increase and multiply and replenish and *subdue* the Earth." Great Britain, in contrast, sought to keep it as "a wilderness of savage hunters" merely as a way "to check, and control and defeat the progress of [American] prosperity [and] to stunt our natural growth."[21]

Adams worried that the new president would retreat in his negotiations with the British, despite the Democratic platform and Polk's renewed declarations "of the unquestionable title of the United States to the whole Oregon country to latitude 54°40' " in his inaugural address and first annual message. During the congressional session of 1845–1846, he threw his failing energies into bolstering Polk's resolve by speaking in support of American claims and voting for a resolution urging the president to give the twelve months' notice of the end of joint occupancy that was required by the Anglo-American convention. Early in the session, however, Adams correctly concluded that the administration would "finish by accepting" a line at the 49th parallel. A number of factors contributed to the signing of a treaty based upon what Adams termed a "compromise" that "can never be yielded with my consent." First, Polk, in Adams's view, mishandled the negotiations by renewing the offer of the 49th parallel. Second, the administration seemed halfhearted about acquiring more land to the north for free states, even as it pushed Mexico for more land to the south. Northern interests received a further blow when the Anglo-American negotiations led, as well, to reductions in the tariff on British manufactures imported into the United States. Finally, Polk feared a war with Great Britain. Adams did not want a war either, but insisted that "to ward it off belong[ed] to the hand of Britain's Queen alone." The outbreak of the war with Mexico in April 1846 made a treaty and peace with Great Britain appear essential. Adams had no opportunity to vote against the treaty and, with his attention now fixed upon the war with Mexico, refrained from speaking out against it.[22]

To Adams, the Mexican War was a travesty against morality, the law of nations, and the Constitution. "There is no aspect of right and wrong," he believed, "of which we can claim the benefit in the controversy." The United States had no just cause of war against Mexico, despite the damage claims of its merchants and the disputed border with Texas. Instead, the administration had deliberately provoked Mexico into war as part of a "design . . . to dismember Mexico, and to annex to the United States not only Texas, but several of her adjoining Provinces on this side [of] the Continent and the Californias on the other side" that dated "at least" to 1830. Jackson, Van Buren, Tyler, and Polk had pursued this goal in ways that gave Mexico "ample cause of War, in self defense, against the United States." By sending a detachment of troops under General Zachary Taylor to the north bank of the Rio Grande in early 1846, Polk, in Adams's view, had committed "an act of flagrant War." Mexico responded as Polk had intended, by crossing the river and engaging Taylor's forces in the disputed zone between Texas and Mexico. The president had already written a war message based upon the damage claims, but, before he could send it to Congress, the news arrived from the Rio Grande. Instead of asking Congress to declare war, Polk asked it simply to recognize that a state of war already existed because of an act of Mexico, which, Adams argued, was "in direct and notorious violation of the truth." The result, in Adams's view, was the effective subversion of the constitutional provision that gave Congress the power to declare war.[23]

Old, tired, and increasingly infirm, Adams could do little to fight the juggernaut created by what he saw as Polk's harnessing of "the spirit of aggrandizement which [had] taken possession of [all of the American] people" to the interests of Southern slaveholders. Polk's war bill charged through both houses of Congress in just two days, with very little time allowed for speeches either for or against it. Still, Adams was one of just fourteen Northern Whigs in the House who voted against what he described as a "most unrighteous war." Furthermore, he urged younger men, such as his son Charles, William Henry Seward, and Charles Sumner, to carry on the battle for him, calling upon them to "Persevere" against the war. While he voted for the appropriations necessary to supply the troops in the field, Adams always voted against commendations, decorations, and resolutions of thanks for the officers who waged it. He also supported every resolution that called for a quick peace without any indemnity or territorial cession from Mexico. His opposition to the war grew deeper after Pennsylvania Democrat David Wilmot offered an amendment to a military appropriations bill that would have prohibited slavery in any territory acquired in the war. Adams initially viewed the Wilmot Proviso as unnecessary, since slavery had already been abolished in Mexico. When he witnessed the intensity of Southern opposition, however, he recognized its importance. Even though it was clear that the South had the votes to defeat it in the Senate, Adams voted for the proviso every time that it came before the House.[24]

Alarmed at the prospects of the Mexican War, Adams battled against it to the very end of his life. In late December 1847, just two months before his death, he wrote to Albert Gallatin: "It is not difficult to foresee what its ultimate issue will be to the people of Mexico, but what it will be to the People of the United States is beyond my foresight, and I turn my eyes away from it." Mexico would lose California, New Mexico, and whatever else the administration demanded. But could the United States absorb this new territory without inflaming sectional tensions, igniting a civil war, sacrificing its republican institutions, or launching a career of empire? On February 20, 1848, news arrived in Washington that a peace treaty, of uncertain terms, had been signed with Mexico. The next morning, Adams cast his final vote against a motion to vote upon a resolution of commendation and thanks for various generals. As the clerk of the House read the text and Adams awaited his turn to vote against the resolution itself, the former president and longtime congressman struggled to rise and then collapsed at his desk.

With whispers of "Mr. Adams is dying!" spreading through the chamber, the House quickly adjourned; the Senate and the Supreme Court also rose as soon as the news reached them. Adams was carried first to the front of the House chamber, then to the Rotunda, then to the east portico, and finally to the Speaker's chamber. There, he revived slightly and called for his old friend, Henry Clay, who came immediately. Before his wife could arrive, he collapsed into a coma; two days later, he died, still lying in the Capitol building.[25]

In the last years of his life, particularly during the Tyler and Polk presidencies, Adams's approach to foreign policy became almost reflexively anti-Southern. Convinced that Southerners had seized the federal government and subverted the basic principles of the American union, Adams tended to oppose anything that would benefit the South. As a result, he rejected otherwise reasonable policies on a number of issues. Perhaps the most striking case was the Oregon boundary, where Adams was willing to risk war with Great Britain rather than join Polk in accepting a line that he himself had offered decades earlier. It was not just specific policy questions upon which Adams reversed himself, however. He also abandoned long-held views about basic aspects of the policymaking process, seemingly without recognizing that he had done so. Having long viewed executive branch control and secrecy as essential for successful diplomacy, he now saw them as evidence of a conspiracy. Having long believed that a treaty could legitimately transfer a territory as vast as the Louisiana Purchase, he now denied that one could transfer Texas. And, having long condemned the provision that gave the power to declare war "exclusively to Congress," he now celebrated it as one of the most important elements of the Constitution.[26]

~

The final stage of Adams's life, his years of retirement and in Congress, found him in an unaccustomed role—as an outsider in the policymaking process and, generally, a critic of the policies themselves. This oppositional stance resulted not from any real change in Adams himself, he firmly believed, but from a sweeping and sudden transformation in the fundamental goals, methods, and assumptions of American policymaking. Adams remained a steadfast proponent of a permanent federal union and an energetic general government, while Jackson, Van Buren, Tyler, and Polk abandoned the principles that had guided American policymakers since the late 1780s. Discovering in their statements and actions a design to perpetuate slavery, favor Southern interests, and entrench the political power of a slaveholding minority, he concluded that the union—and the republican system that it made possible—was in grave danger. He fought this design on various fronts: the "gag rule," the annexation of Texas, the Oregon border, and the Mexican War. Northerners increasingly called him "Old Man Eloquent"— champion of their rights and foe of slavery. Southerners viewed him very differently; in the last decade of his life, he received many letters from Southerners threatening, as one put it, "to cut [his] throat from ear to Ear." Combined with his conviction that the very future of his country was at stake, such hatred only fueled a political combativeness that kept him fighting to the very end. Begged by his wife to stay home from the House on a day when he felt unwell in the last weeks of his life, Adams "answered as usual that if he *did* he should *die!*" "He [could not] live without excitement," as Louisa Catherine perceptively noted, "it [had] become a habit."[27]

Notes

1. John Quincy Adams (hereafter JQA), diary entry, December 31, 1828, *Memoirs of John Quincy Adams: Comprising Portions of His Diary from 1795 to 1848*, ed. Charles Francis Adams, 12 vols. (Philadelphia, 1874–1877), 8:88 (hereafter *Memoirs*).

2. JQA to Charles Francis Adams, May 24, 1836, Adams Papers, Massachusetts Historical Society, Boston (microfilm), reel 152 (hereafter Adams Papers).

3. JQA, diary entry, May 13, 1827, *Memoirs*, 7:273.

4. JQA to William Plumer, March 16, 1829, Adams Papers, reel 149.

5. JQA, diary entry, September 22, 1830, *Memoirs*, 8:241; JQA, diary entry, November 7, 1830, ibid., 246, 245, 247.

6. JQA to Charles W. Upham, February 2, 1837, Edward H. Tatum Jr., ed., "Ten Unpublished Letters of John Quincy Adams, 1796–1837," *Huntington Library Quarterly* 4 (April 1941): 382 (hereafter "Ten Unpublished Letters"); JQA to Charles Francis Adams, March 8, 1829, Adams Papers, reel 148; JQA, diary entry, May 22, 1830, *Memoirs*, 8:229; JQA to Samuel L. Southard, June 6, 1830, Adams Papers, reel 150; JQA, diary entry, July 30, 1834, *Memoirs*, 9:162.

7. JQA to Robert Walsh, April 16, 1836, Adams Papers, reel 152; JQA, *An Oration Addressed to the Citizens of the Town of Quincy, on the Fourth of July, 1831, the Fifty-fifth Anniversary of the Independence of the United States of America* (Boston, 1831), 36; JQA to Henry Clay, September 7, 1831, *The Papers of Henry Clay*, ed. James F. Hopkins et al., 10 vols. and Supplement (Lexington, Ky., 1959–1992), 8:397 (hereafter *Papers of Clay*); JQA to Benjamin Vaughan, September 9, 1831, Adams Papers, reel 150.

8. JQA, diary entry, January 28, 1802, *Memoirs*, 1:249.

9. JQA, diary entry, December 28, 1831, ibid., 8:447; JQA to Morton Eddy, May 1, 1836, Adams Papers, reel 152.

10. JQA to Charles Francis Adams, May 24, 1836, Adams Papers, reel 152; JQA, diary entry, July 30, 1834, *Memoirs*, 9:162; JQA, diary entry, February 22, 1832, ibid., 8:479; JQA, diary entry, July 30, 1834, ibid., 9:162. Adams began the letter to his son by referring to the French philosopher Jean-Jacques Rousseau, who "in the last years of his life was tortured by an imagination that the whole human race without a single exception were leagued together in a conspiracy for his destruction." "I am not yet quite come to that," Adams insisted.

11. JQA, diary entry, January 10, 1820, *Memoirs*, 4.502; JQA to Benjamin Waterhouse, October 15, 1835, Adams Papers, reel 152; JQA to Benjamin Lundy, March 11, 1838, ibid., reel 153.

12. JQA, diary entry, March 3, 1820, *Memoirs*, 5:11, 4, 11; JQA, diary entry, February 23, 1820, ibid., 4:530; JQA, diary entry, February 24, 1820, ibid., 4:531.

13. JQA, diary entry, April 15, 1837, ibid., 9:349; JQA, diary entry, August 22, 1835, ibid., 259; JQA, diary entry, April 15, 1837, ibid., 350, 349; JQA, speech of May 25, 1836, *Register of Debates in Congress*, 24 Cong., 1st sess., vol. 12, part 4, 4047.

14. JQA to William E. Channing, November 21, 1837, Adams Papers, reel 153.

15. Ibid.; JQA to Charles Francis Adams, May 24, 1836, ibid., reel 152; JQA to Alexander H. Everett, May 10, 1836, Andrew C. McLaughlin, ed., "Letters of John Quincy Adams to Alexander H. Everett, 1811–1837," *American Historical Review* 11 (January 1906): 350, 351; JQA to William E. Channing, November 21, 1837, Adams Papers, reel 153.

16. JQA to Charles Francis Adams, May 24, 1836, Adams Papers, reel 152; JQA to William E. Channing, November 21, 1837, ibid., reel 153.

17. JQA, diary entry, December 5, 1837, *Memoirs*, 9:441; JQA to Timothy Pitkin, April 22, 1837, "Ten Unpublished Letters," 388; JQA to William E. Channing, November 21, 1837, Adams Papers, reel 153.

18. JQA, diary entry, April 4, 1841, *Memoirs*, 10:457; JQA to Richard Rush, October 16, 1845, Adams Papers, reel 154.

19. JQA, diary entry, June 10, 1844, *Memoirs*, 12:49.

20. Ibid.; JQA, address of October 1845, quoted in Samuel Flagg Bemis, *John Quincy Adams and the Union* (New York, 1956), 474; JQA, diary entry, February 19, 1845, *Memoirs*, 12:171; JQA, diary entry, February 28, 1845, ibid., 173.

21. JQA, diary entry, December 14, 1845, *Memoirs*, 12:221; JQA, diary entry, February 19, 1845, ibid., 171; JQA to Joseph Sturge, April 1846, Adams Papers, reel 155.

22. JQA, diary entry, December 14, 1845, *Memoirs*, 12:220, 221; JQA to Joseph Sturge, April 1846, Adams Papers, reel 155.

23. JQA to Brantz Mayer, July 6, 1847, Adams Papers, reel 155; JQA to Albert Gallatin, December 26, 1847, ibid.

24. JQA, diary entry, February 14, 1846, *Memoirs*, 12:247; JQA, diary entry, May 11, 1846, ibid., 263; JQA to Charles Francis Adams, June 29, 1846, Adams Papers, reel 155.

25. JQA to Albert Gallatin, December 26, 1847, Adams Papers, reel 155; account of H. B. Stanton, February 21, 1848, quoted in Bemis, *John Quincy Adams and the Union*, 535.

26. JQA to Albert Gallatin, December 26, 1847, Adams Papers, reel 155.

27. Peter Longate to JQA, February 27, 1839, quoted in Bemis, *John Quincy Adams and the Union*, 376; Louisa Catherine Adams, diary entry, February 3, 1848, in her letter to Abigail Brooks Adams, January 27–February 4, 1848, Adams Papers, reel 537.

Conclusion

Was John Quincy Adams the "greatest" American secretary of state? Answering this question fairly would require comparing him to the other sixty-two men and one woman who have also held the office. Rather than asking if he was the "greatest," we might simply ask if he was "great." It seems clear that his service as secretary of state and, more generally, as a foreign policymaker was mixed. Failures counterbalanced successes; if the latter appear more important in retrospect, it may simply be because it is easier for us to see the impact of things that did happen (such as the Transcontinental Treaty) than things that did not (such as the slave trade convention). As secretary of state and even as president, moreover, Adams never fully controlled the making and implementing of foreign policy in the way that we might consider necessary for greatness. His strongest claim to greatness, however, may well rest on his ability to achieve so much despite the constraints imposed by the nation's federal and republican system. Adams understood that he could not exercise the kind of control over foreign relations enjoyed by his "great" European contemporaries and often managed to use these very limitations for the nation's benefit.

What were Adams's major successes during the fifteen years of his greatest influence, between the negotiations at Ghent in 1814 and the end of his presidency in 1829? Perhaps his single greatest achievement as a foreign policymaker in this period was an invisible one—preserving peace for the present and reducing tensions for the future. At a time when the United States seemed especially weak and fragile and the international system appeared especially volatile and hostile, Adams—along with James Madison, James Monroe, and other leading policymakers—clearly recognized the importance of peace. Driven by his conviction that any war would "necessarily plac[e] high interests of different portions of the Union in conflict with each other, and thereby [endanger] the Union itself," Adams helped to shape policies that peacefully resolved or simply postponed potentially explosive conflicts with Great

Britain, Spain, Russia, and France. Most important, he dramatically reduced the likelihood of war with the nation's most dangerous enemy. Having entered the postwar era believing that future wars with Great Britain were certain and imminent, Adams recognized and encouraged developments in Europe and the New World that tended to separate Great Britain from the European monarchies and to foster a "coincidence of principle[s]" with the American republic. Adams's success in this area was so complete as to obscure the very difficulty of the undertaking; for years, historians viewed the post-War of 1812 period as an "era of free security," a concept that would have been totally unimaginable to Madison, Monroe, and Adams at the time.[1]

Adams also succeeded in promoting territorial and commercial expansion during these years. Numerous treaties, conventions, and informal agreements with various European and American powers testify to his achievement. His commercial negotiations secured expanded access and improved terms for American merchants, even if they did not generally extend as far as he hoped. His territorial negotiations served a number of purposes beyond merely acquiring more land for the United States. By bolstering American claims in the Oregon country through his negotiations with Great Britain, Russia, and, especially, Spain, Adams fostered American trade throughout the Pacific. By settling or deferring territorial disputes with these powers, moreover, he eliminated sources of conflict or war. Confident that "in the natural course of events we must outgrow all the obstacles which European powers [were] so desirous of opposing to us," Adams understood "that in all our negotiations upon this subject our interest was to gain time." Such patience furthered not only the immediate policy of preserving the peace but also the overall goal of strengthening the union. Acquiring and incorporating new territory in a gradual fashion would help to encourage a "tendency [in] our popular sentiments [that] was increasingly towards union." Adams trusted that, in time, more and more Americans would think, as he did, that "a Government by federation [was] practicable upon a territory as extensive as this continent."[2]

Offsetting these successes, at least to some degree, were various failures. Many of Adams's efforts fell short of his goals. He never managed to bring foreign policymaking under his control in the way that he had planned when he entered the State Department. As a result, he frequently found himself hurriedly responding to developments that he had not expected rather than deliberately wielding the inducements and threats of diplomacy. Furthermore, his commercial agreements did not generally include the desired principle of reciprocity. His negotiations with France led to a convention that openly defied this principle by accepting discriminatory duties, while his pressures upon Great Britain resulted in the closure of British colonial ports to American ships and produce. The slave trade convention with the British never took effect. And Adams's dream of a convention to protect private property in wartime was never even discussed. At the same time, his policies toward Spanish America rarely brought the intended results. Adams avoided embroiling the United States in a war with Spain, but neither recognizing the new states, nor announcing the Monroe Doctrine, nor accepting the invitation to the Panama Congress succeeded in establishing the American model of national independence, republican government, and liberal commerce in the New World. Instead, his ultimate response to Spanish American independence during his presidency showed the limits of the American commitment to union as a solution to the problem of neighborhood in international relations. Although he believed that nothing but a single political union could secure his basic goals, he nonetheless rejected both a hemispheric union and a separate Latin American union.

To Adams, these shortcomings paled in comparison to his much more significant failure to establish permanently his commitment to using the energy of the government to improve the lives of the American people and perpetuate the federal union. By the time of his election to the presidency, he later explained, this "system of Government for the Union" seemed fully "established." Over the next four years, the rise of the Democrats and the election of Andrew Jackson presented a new challenge driven by "the perverting and crafty Jeffersonian paradoxes of State rights and Nullification." But Adams still trusted, in the final days before he left the presidency, that "the cause of Union and of improvement [would] remain." The administrations of Jackson and his successors, Democrat and Whig, over the remainder of Adams's life showed clearly that this "cause" would not again receive the attention and commitment that he thought it required. After learning in the spring of 1836 that a French statesman had translated and published his inaugural address and first annual message to Congress "as expositions of the American system of Government," Adams insisted: "it was only *my* system." As he saw it, under Jackson, this system had quickly "been superseded" by measures that were inimical to it, including "Bank and Indian Wars, Nullification, Tariff compromises, [and] the surrender of Colonial Trade." "The great object of my life . . . as applied to the administration of the Government of the United States," Adams explained the following year, "has *failed*." The future "prospect" for the United States under the constricted vision of his successors had "blasted all the high aspirations of [his] younger days."[3]

In his increasingly dark assessments of the nation's future during his final years, Adams might have traced the aftereffects of both his successes and his failures. His successful efforts at territorial and commercial expansion had fueled "the spirit of aggrandizement" in the American people and government that he feared would "hereafter characterize their history." "The North American continent and the archipelago of islands separating it from the Southern continent," he sarcastically predicted in the months before the Mexican War, "must, and will in no great distance of time, form component parts of this great confederated Anglo-Saxon republic." Adams worried that, in the course of this rapid expansion, the United States would find it impossible to remain either "confederated" or a "republic." Either the federal union would dissolve as it attempted to solve the slavery question in its new territories, or its republican government would produce "a race of Caesars to subdue [South America]" in order to extend the empire even further.[4]

At the same time, his failure to establish permanently the system of using federal energy to strengthen the union resulted from and contributed to a union-threatening consolidation of political power in the hands of slaveholding Southerners and their Northern allies. Adams's successors largely abandoned the general approach to policymaking that had guided his predecessors for four decades and increasingly questioned the value of union itself. Unable, in the final battles of his life, to arrest the growing influence of the "slave power," Adams grew more and more fearful that his dreams of a perpetual union were imperiled by the struggle between slavery and freedom. "Slavery," he feared, would "be the destined sword in the hand of the destroying angel which is to sever the ties of this Union." As early as the Missouri Crisis, Adams had found a glimmer of hope in this most dreadful of all prospects. "A dissolution of the Union for the cause of slavery," he correctly predicted more than four decades before the Civil War, "would be followed by a servile war in the slave-holding States, combined with a war between the two severed portions of the Union." He trusted that the final result would "be the extirpation of slavery from this whole continent; and, calamitous and desolating as this course of events in its progress must be, so glorious would be its final issue, that, as God shall judge me, I dare not say that it is not to be desired." Adams did not live to see either the awful civil war that he so dreaded or the total emancipation that he could only hope would be its redeeming outcome.[5]

Finding it necessary to identify his own accomplishments in October 1824 as part of the presidential election campaign, Adams included the Treaty of Ghent, the conventions of 1815 and 1818 with Great Britain, the Transcontinental Treaty with Spain, the commercial convention of 1822 with France, the northwest boundary convention with Russia, and the slave trade convention. We might want to remove from this list the convention with France, which had been signed only over his staunch opposition, and the slave trade convention, which never took effect. But we might want to add the Rush-Bagot Agreement of 1817, the recognition of the Spanish American states, and, given its later significance, his role in the Monroe Doctrine. Of course, there were many other important accomplishments both before 1814 and after 1824. Adams may not have achieved all that he planned and may have assigned grave consequences to his shortcomings. But few policymakers understood the distinct nature of the American political system as well as he did. And few individuals left as great a mark on American foreign policy as John Quincy Adams, both while secretary of state and during a long life in politics.

Notes

1. John Quincy Adams (hereafter JQA), diary entry, December 2, 1823, *Memoirs of John Quincy Adams: Comprising Portions of His Diary from 1795 to 1848*, ed. Charles Francis Adams, 12 vols. (Philadelphia, 1874–1877), 6:224 (hereafter *Memoirs*); JQA, diary entry, June 20, 1823, ibid., 152; C. Vann Woodward, "The Age of Reinterpretation," *American Historical Review* 66 (October 1960): 3.

2. JQA, diary entry, December 26, 1824, *Memoirs*, 6:454; JQA, diary entry, March 9, 1824, ibid., 251.

3. JQA to Henry Clay, September 20, 1842, *The Papers of Henry Clay*, ed. James F. Hopkins et al., 10 vols. and Supplement (Lexington, Ky., 1959–1992), 9:769; JQA, diary entry, "Day" [February 1829], *Memoirs*, 8:101; JQA to Robert Walsh, April 16, 1836, Adams Papers, Massachusetts Historical Society, Boston (microfilm), reel 152 (hereafter Adams Papers); JQA to Charles W. Upham, February 2, 1837, Edward H. Tatum Jr., ed., "Ten

Unpublished Letters of John Quincy Adams, 1796–1837," *Huntington Library Quarterly* 4 (April 1941): 383.

4. JQA, diary entry, February 14, 1846, *Memoirs*, 12:247; JQA to Richard Rush, October 16, 1845, Adams Papers, reel 154.

5. JQA, diary entry, November 29, 1820, *Memoirs*, 5:210.

Bibliographic Essay

This essay aims to include only the most important primary and secondary sources for a study of John Quincy Adams's life, policies, and times. Students and scholars who are interested in undertaking a more thorough investigation should begin with two more comprehensive bibliographies: Kenneth V. Jones, ed., *John Quincy Adams, 1767–1848: Chronology, Documents, Bibliographical Aids* (Dobbs Ferry, N.Y., 1970); and Lynn H. Parsons, comp., *John Quincy Adams: A Bibliography* (Westport, Conn., 1993). Many of the arguments advanced and topics addressed in this book are developed at greater length and from a broader perspective in my *The American Union and the Problem of Neighborhood: The United States and the Collapse of the Spanish Empire, 1783–1829* (Chapel Hill, N.C., 1998). As such, its bibliography would be useful for anyone interested in unionist thought, the War of 1812, and the American response to the dissolution of the Spanish empire from the Louisiana Purchase through the Panama Congress.

John Quincy Adams left an extensive body of primary sources: diaries, letterbooks, incoming correspondence, and published and unpublished writings. Much of this material is accessible in the microfilmed collection of Adams Papers from the Massachusetts Historical Society, which covers four generations of the family beginning with John and Abigail. Most of the official letters written and received by Adams in his various diplomatic positions are also available on microfilm in various parts of Record Group 59 (General Records of the Department of State) of the National Archives. But some critical correspondence from his tenure as secretary of state can be found in the James Monroe Papers of the Library of Congress and the New York Public Library (both of these collections have also been microfilmed).

The Massachusetts Historical Society is gradually publishing some of the key elements of its collection. Fully annotated and complete editions of Adams's diary and family correspondence will be published eventually. At this time, however, David Grayson Allen et al., eds., *Diary of John Quincy Adams*, 2 vols. to date (Cambridge, Mass., 1981–), and L. H. Butterfield et al., eds., *Adams Family Correspondence*, 6 vols. to date (Cambridge, Mass., 1963–), extend no further than the 1790s. As a result, scholars must continue to make use of the older, incomplete, and generally unannotated editions: Charles Francis Adams, ed., *Memoirs of John Quincy Adams: Comprising Portions of His Diary from 1795 to 1848*, 12 vols. (Philadelphia, 1874–1877); and Worthington Chauncey Ford, ed., *Writings of John Quincy Adams*, 7 vols. (New York, 1913–1917). The *Memoirs* include only about half of the material in Adams's diaries, but Charles Francis rarely withheld his father's comments on political matters (and clearly marked what he published on the originals). The *Writings* are much more limited, printing only Adams's end of the correspondence and extending only to the summer of 1823.

Some of the most important documents concerning some of the most critical policy issues dealt with by Adams over the course of his diplomatic service have also been published. Selected documents from both the American and Russian sides can be found in Nina N. Bashkina and Nikolai Bolkhovitinov et al., eds., *The United States and Russia: The Beginning of Relations, 1765–1815* (Washington, D.C., 1980). Similarly, both American and British documents regarding boundaries, fisheries, the Great Lakes, and other issues are published in William R. Manning, ed., *Diplomatic Correspondence of the United States: Canadian Relations, 1784–1860*, 4 vols. (Washington, D.C., 1940–1945). And documents from a number of Latin American nations, the major European powers, and the United States are collected in William R. Manning, ed., *Diplomatic Correspondence of the United States Concerning the Independence of the Latin-American Nations*, 3 vols. (New York, 1925). Worthington C. Ford published a collection of internal correspondence and draft memoranda from the policy debates of the fall of 1823 as "Some Original Documents on the Genesis of the Monroe Doctrine," *Proceedings of the Massachusetts Historical Society* 2d ser., 15 (January 1902): 373–436.

In the century and a half since his death, John Quincy Adams has had countless biographers. Two of the best general studies are the most recent: Paul C. Nagel, *John Quincy Adams: A Public Life, A Private Life* (New York, 1997); and Lynn Hudson Parsons, *John Quincy Adams* (Madison, Wisc., 1997). Despite his subtitle, Nagel slights Adams's public life in favor of his private life, in which he finds evidence of "a major depression that dogged Adams's life"

(p. xi). Parsons's work provides more balanced coverage. Nagel has also written helpful histories of the Adams family (*Descent from Glory* [New York, 1983]) and the Adams women (*The Adams Women* [New York, 1987]). The long and often-troubled relationship between John Quincy and Louisa Catherine is also well covered in Jack Shepherd, *Cannibals of the Heart: A Personal Biography of Louisa Catherine and John Quincy Adams* (New York, 1980).

Anyone interested in Adams's foreign policy must begin with two volumes by Samuel Flagg Bemis (the first scholar to have full access to the unpublished Adams Papers). The first, *John Quincy Adams and the Foundations of American Foreign Policy* (New York, 1949), ends with Adams's presidency and focuses upon foreign policy. The second, *John Quincy Adams and the Union* (New York, 1956), begins with Adams's presidency and concentrates upon his growing fears about slavery and sectionalism. Later scholars have revised many of Bemis's arguments, but none have approached the comprehensiveness of his work. Useful studies of Adams's foreign policy thinking include: Norman A. Graebner, "John Quincy Adams and the Federalist Tradition," in *Foundations of American Foreign Policy: A Realist Appraisal from Franklin to McKinley* (Wilmington, Del., 1985), 145–79; and Stanley J. Underdal, "John Quincy Adams and American Continental Expansion," *Journal of the West* 31 (July 1992): 27–37. Political scientist Greg Russell has written extensively on the importance of morality and virtue in Adams's policymaking. See his "The Ethics of Power in American Diplomacy: The State-craft of John Quincy Adams," *Review of Politics* 52 (Winter 1990): 3–31 (with Daniel G. Lang); *John Quincy Adams and the Public Virtues of Diplomacy* (Columbia, Mo., 1995); and "John Quincy Adams: Virtue and the Tragedy of the Statesman," *New England Quarterly* 69 (March 1996): 56–74.

Adams's upbringing is well covered in most of the general biographies. But the decade between his return from Europe and his entry into the diplomatic service is the particular topic of Robert A. East, *John Quincy Adams: The Critical Years, 1785–1794* (New York, 1962). The Massachusetts background that encouraged him to expect government to work for the improvement of citizens is fully developed in two works: Oscar Handlin and Mary Flug Handlin, *Commonwealth: A Study of the Role of Government in the American Economy: Massachusetts, 1774–1861* (New York, 1947); and Stephen Innes, *Creating the Commonwealth: The Economic Culture of Puritan New England* (New York, 1995). The idea of gentility, and John Adams's thoughts on this subject, in late colonial and revolutionary America is elaborated in Richard L. Bushman, *The Refinement of America: Persons, Houses, Cities* (New York, 1992).

A number of recent studies have highlighted the Founders' fears of the effects of disunion in explaining the origins of the Constitution. Of particular importance are the works of Peter S. Onuf, including: *The Origins of the Federal Republic: Jurisdictional Controversies in the United States, 1775–1787* (Philadelphia, 1983); "State Sovereignty and the Making of the Constitution," in *Conceptual Change and the Constitution*, ed. Terence Ball and J. G. A. Pocock (Lawrence, Kans., 1988), 78–98; and "Anarchy and the Crisis of the Union," in *To Form a More Perfect Union: The Critical Ideas of the Constitution*, ed. Herman Belz et al. (Charlottesville, Va., 1992), 272–302. The vast literature on the Founding was reviewed by Onuf in "Reflections on the Founding: Constitutional Historiography in Bicentennial Perspective," *William and Mary Quarterly* 3d ser., 46 (April 1989): 341–75. In *The Union As It Is: Constitutional Unionism and Sectional Compromise, 1787–1861* (Chapel Hill, N.C., 1991), Peter B. Knupfer has described the continuing importance of these concerns, particularly in Congress. And Peter Onuf and Nicholas Onuf have situated American federalism within contemporary, Enlightenment thinking about international relations in their *Federal Union, Modern World: The Law of Nations in an Age of Revolution, 1776–1814* (Madison, Wisc., 1993).

The political divisions of the 1790s that led Adams to adopt the Founders' logic for the union have long held the attention of historians and political scientists. The best general surveys of this decade are: James Roger Sharp, *American Politics in the Early Republic: The New Nation in Crisis* (New Haven, Conn., 1993), which emphasizes the fragility of the union; and Stanley Elkins and Eric McKitrick, *The Age of Federalism: The Early American Republic, 1788–1800* (New York, 1993), which tilts strongly in favor of Alexander Hamilton and the Federalists. Two important studies that develop (in contradictory ways) the policy impact of conflicting Federalist and Republican ideas about economic and social development are: Drew R. McCoy, *The Elusive Republic: Political Economy in Jeffersonian America* (Chapel Hill, N.C., 1980); and John R. Nelson Jr., *Liberty and Property: Political Economy and Policymaking in the New Nation, 1789–1812* (Baltimore, Md., 1987). The context in which Adams initially sided with the Federalists is well covered in James M. Banner Jr., *To the Hartford Convention: The Federalists and the Origins of Party Politics in Massachusetts, 1789–1815* (New York, 1970). David Hackett Fischer, *The Revolution of American Conservatism: The Federalist Party in the Era of Jeffersonian Democracy* (New York, 1965), and Linda K. Kerber, *Federalists in Dissent: Imagery and Ideology in Jeffersonian America* (Ithaca, N.Y., 1970), carry the story of the Federalist party into the era of Jeffersonian ascendency after 1801. Adams's gradual break with the party over the course of Thomas Jefferson's presidency is examined in Robert R. Thompson, "John Quincy Adams, Apostate: From 'Outrageous Federalist' to 'Republican Exile,' 1801–1809," *Journal of the Early Republic* 11 (Summer 1991): 161–83.

The foreign policymaking of the Jefferson administration has been most recently assessed (generally unfavorably) by Robert W. Tucker and David C. Hendrickson, *Empire of Liberty: The Statecraft of Thomas Jefferson* (New York, 1990), and (generally favorably) by Lawrence S. Kaplan, *Thomas Jefferson: Westward the Course of Empire* (Wilmington, Del., 1998). Valuable discussions of the crisis over French control of the lower Mississippi River that ended with the Louisiana Purchase include: Arthur Preston Whitaker, *The Mississippi Question, 1795–1803: A Study in Trade, Politics, and Diplomacy* (New York, 1934); Alexander DeConde, *This Affair of Louisiana* (New York, 1976); and Peter S. Onuf, "The Expanding Union," in *Devising Liberty: The Conditions of Freedom in the Early American Republic*, ed. David T. Konig (Stanford, Calif., 1995), 50–80. Federalist opposition to the purchase is described and explained in Michael Allen, "The Federalists and the West, 1783–1803," *Western Pennsylvania Historical Magazine* 61 (October 1978): 315–32; Gerald H. Clarfield, *Timothy Pickering and the American Republic* (Pittsburgh, Pa., 1980); Paul A. Varg, *New England and Foreign Relations, 1789–1850* (Hanover, N.H., 1983); and Reginald Horsman, "The Dimensions of an 'Empire for Liberty': Expansion and Republicanism, 1775–1825," *Journal of the Early Republic* 9 (Spring 1989): 1–20. Clarfield and Varg also discuss the secessionist plot developed by some New England Federalists during the winter of 1803–1804.

Adams's final break with the Federalists came in response to the Embargo. The logic behind and wisdom of this policy has been debated at great length through the years. The works by Tucker and Hendrickson and Kaplan offer their assessments amidst their general accounts of Jeffersonian foreign policy. The Embargo is also the particular subject of Burton Spivak, *Jefferson's English Crisis: Commerce, Embargo, and the Republican Revolution* (Charlottesville, Va., 1979). The violations of the Embargo that so impressed Adams have been studied in countless localities from New England to Georgia. Adams experienced them most directly in Boston, where they are nicely described by: Robin D. S. Higham, "The Port of

Boston and the Embargo of 1807–1809," *American Neptune* 16 (July 1956): 189–210; and Douglas Lamar Jones, "'The Caprice of Juries': The Enforcement of the Jeffersonian Embargo in Massachusetts," *American Journal of Legal History* 24 (October 1980): 307–30. The problems of enforcement, as experienced by the administration in Washington, are detailed in Richard Mannix, "Gallatin, Jefferson, and the Embargo of 1808," *Diplomatic History* 3 (Spring 1979): 151–72.

In the first weeks of James Madison's presidency, Adams accepted a posting in Russia. The general background of Russo-American relations throughout this period is provided by Nikolai Bolkhovitinov, *The Beginnings of Russian-American Relations, 1775–1815* (Cambridge, Mass., 1975), and Norman E. Saul, *Distant Friends: The United States and Russia, 1763–1867* (Lawrence, Kans., 1991). Adams spent much of his time in St. Petersburg dealing with commercial issues. The context of these negotiations is recounted in Alfred W. Crosby Jr., *America, Russia, Hemp, and Napoleon: American Trade with Russia and the Baltic, 1783–1812* (Columbus, Ohio, 1965); Adams's own efforts, both at the time and subsequently, are the focus of David W. McFadden, "John Quincy Adams, American Commercial Diplomacy, and Russia, 1809–1825," *New England Quarterly* 66 (December 1993): 613–29. For an interesting sidelight on this phase of Adams's life, see also Catherine Allgor, " 'A Republican in a Monarchy': Louisa Catherine Adams in Russia," *Diplomatic History* 21 (Winter 1997): 15–43.

While Adams served in Russia, his nation struggled through the trying War of 1812. The war itself is well covered by J. C. A. Stagg, *Mr. Madison's War: Politics, Diplomacy, and Warfare in the Early American Republic, 1783–1830* (Princeton, N.J., 1983), and Donald R. Hickey, *The War of 1812: A Forgotten Conflict* (Urbana, Ill., 1989). The problems that undermined the Madison administration's prosecution of the war are fully detailed by Stagg. The concerns that led New England Federalists to the Hartford Convention receive careful treatment in the book by Banner cited above, as well as in Hickey's "New England's Defense Problem and the Genesis of the Hartford Convention," *New England Quarterly* 50 (December 1977): 587–604. The Ghent negotiations that ended the war are discussed, with a particular interest in Adams's role, in Bradford Perkins, *Castlereagh and Adams: England and the United States, 1812–1823* (Berkeley, Calif., 1964), which is one of the key books on Adams's policymaking during his years of greatest influence.

In the immediate aftermath of the War of 1812, the Madison administration joined with Congress to redress the nation's lack of military preparedness in various ways. These measures begin George Dangerfield's *The Awakening of American Nationalism, 1815–1828* (New York, 1965) and close Robert Allen Rutland's *The Presidency of James Madison* (Lawrence, Kans., 1990), but are best explained in Michael Stuart Fitzgerald's "'Nature Unsubdued': Diplomacy, Expansion and the American Military Buildup of 1815–1816," *Mid-America* 77 (Winter 1995): 5–32. The new conditions in Europe that heightened the American sense of insecurity are described in Alan Sked, ed., *Europe's Balance of Power, 1815–1848* (New York, 1979), and F. R. Bridge and Roger Bullen, *The Great Powers and the European States System, 1815–1914* (London, 1980), as well as in two older works on the European context of the Monroe Doctrine: W. P. Cresson, *The Holy Alliance: The European Background of the Monroe Doctrine* (New York, 1922); and Edward Howland Tatum Jr., *The United States and Europe, 1815–1823: A Study in the Background of the Monroe Doctrine* (Berkeley, Calif., 1936).

The best general overviews of the administration of James Monroe are Dangerfield's *Awakening of American Nationalism* and *The Era of Good Feelings* (New York, 1952) and Noble E. Cunningham Jr.'s *The Presidency of James Monroe* (Lawrence, Kans., 1996). The economic and sectional crises that dominated the second half of Monroe's first term are detailed in Murray N. Rothbard, *The Panic of 1819: Reactions and Policies* (New York, 1962), and Glover Moore, *The Missouri Controversy, 1819–1821* (Lexington, Ky., 1953). Useful biographies of the key men who served with Adams in the administration include: Harry Ammon, *James Monroe: The Quest for National Identity* (New York, 1971); Chase C. Mooney, *William H. Crawford, 1772–1834* (Lexington, Ky., 1974); and John Niven, *John C. Calhoun and the Price of Union: A Biography* (Baton Rouge, La., 1988). The lives of Adams's most important diplomats abroad are discussed in J. H. Powell, *Richard Rush: Republican Diplomat, 1780–1859* (Philadelphia, 1942), and Raymond Walters Jr., *Albert Gallatin: Jeffersonian Financier and Diplomat* (New York, 1957). Robert V. Remini has written biographies of two critical figures in Adams's life: one he considered, first, an ally and, later, an enemy (*Andrew Jackson and the Course of American Empire, 1767–1821* [New York, 1977]); the other he viewed, first, as an enemy, and, later, as an ally (*Henry Clay: Statesman of the Union* [New York, 1991]).

Much of Adams's first term in the State Department focused upon territorial disputes with the nation's British and Spanish neighbors. The Convention of 1818 is well handled by Bemis and Perkins, but a larger context for it is provided by Reginald C. Stuart,

United States Expansionism and British North America, 1775–1871 (Chapel Hill, N.C., 1988). The negotiations with Spain that led to the Transcontinental Treaty are treated by Philip Coolidge Brooks, *Diplomacy and the Borderlands: The Adams-Onís Treaty of 1819* (Berkeley, Calif., 1939), and William Earl Weeks, *John Quincy Adams and American Global Empire* (Lexington, Ky., 1992). Jackson's rampage through Florida, which helped to precipitate the Spanish concessions that led to the treaty, is described in Remini's *Andrew Jackson and the Course of American Empire*, David S. Heidler and Jeanne T. Heidler's *Old Hickory's War: Andrew Jackson and the Quest for Empire* (Mechanicsburg, Pa., 1996), and Frank Lawrence Owsley Jr. and Gene A. Smith's *Filibusters and Expansionists: Jeffersonian Manifest Destiny, 1800–1821* (Tuscaloosa, Ala., 1997).

Other than my own recent book, most of the literature on the U.S. diplomatic response to the dissolution of Spain's New World empire is fairly old. Nonetheless, William Spence Robinson's "The Recognition of the Hispanic American Nations by the United States," *Hispanic American Historical Review* 1 (August 1918): 239–69, Charles C. Griffin's *The United States and the Disruption of the Spanish Empire, 1810–1822: A Study of the Relations of the United States with Spain and with the Rebel Spanish Colonies* (New York, 1937), and, especially, Arthur Preston Whitaker's *The United States and the Independence of Latin America, 1800–1830* (Baltimore, Md., 1941) remain quite useful. Two recent works that examine the American response to Spanish America from a somewhat broader perspective are John J. Johnson's *A Hemisphere Apart: The Foundations of United States Policy toward Latin America* (Baltimore, Md., 1990) and Fredrick B. Pike's *The United States and Latin America: Myths and Stereotypes of Civilization and Nature* (Austin, Tex., 1992). A far-reaching Anglo-American rivalry over markets and influence in Spanish America is depicted by J. Fred Rippy, *Rivalry of the United States and Great Britain Over Latin America, 1808–1830* (Baltimore, Md., 1929), and Kinley Brauer, "The United States and British Imperial Expansion, 1815–60," *Diplomatic History* 12 (Winter 1988): 19–37.

Much of the writing on Adams's second term as secretary of state focuses on the Monroe Doctrine. But Adams also devoted considerable effort to maritime issues. Though old, F. Lee Benns, *The American Struggle for the British West India Carrying Trade, 1815–1830* (Bloomington, Ind., 1923), remains the most thorough study of Anglo-American commercial tensions in a key area. Adams's faltering efforts to suppress the slave trade are placed in context by

W. E. B. DuBois, *The Suppression of the African Slave-Trade to the United States of America, 1638–1870* (New York, 1896), and Hugh G. Soulsby, *The Right of Search and the Slave Trade in Anglo-American Relations, 1814–1862* (Baltimore, Md., 1933). During the same years, Monroe and Adams finally decided to recognize the Spanish American states. This step is discussed in most of the works on the American response to the Spanish American revolutions cited above. Additionally, three articles offer valuable insights into the administration's thinking about Spanish American independence: Charles Wilson Hackett, "The Development of John Quincy Adams's Policy with Respect to an American Confederation and the Panama Congress, 1822–1825," *Hispanic American Historical Review* 8 (November 1928): 496–526; Light T. Cummins, "John Quincy Adams and Latin American Nationalism," *Revista de Historia de América* 86 (Julio–Diciembre 1978): 221–31; and Piero Gleijeses, "The Limits of Sympathy: The United States and the Independence of Spanish America," *Journal of Latin American Studies* 24 (October 1992): 481–505. The Monroe and Adams administrations' troubles with the first set of diplomats sent to the new Latin American nations are recounted in the essays in T. Ray Shurbutt, ed., *United States-Latin American Relations, 1800–1850: The Formative Generations* (Tuscaloosa, Ala., 1991).

A good starting place for understanding the questions raised by and the literature on the Monroe Doctrine is Jerald A. Combs's historiographical essay, "The Origins of the Monroe Doctrine: A Survey of Interpretations by United States Historians," *Australian Journal of Politics and History* 27 (1981): 186–96. The most important of the pre-Combs works include those by Bemis, Perkins, Dangerfield (*Awakening of American Nationalism*), and Whitaker (*United States and the Independence of Latin America*) cited above. For years, the standard interpretation of the Monroe Doctrine and its aftermath appeared in two works by Dexter Perkins, *The Monroe Doctrine, 1823–1826* (Cambridge, Mass., 1927) and *The Monroe Doctrine, 1826–1867* (Baltimore, Md., 1933). The most controversial recent explanation of the Monroe Doctrine is Ernest R. May's *The Making of the Monroe Doctrine* (Cambridge, Mass., 1975), which argues that domestic politics, particularly the election of 1824, shaped the position taken on the Allied threat and the British proposal by each cabinet member. This argument was directly challenged by Monroe's biographer, Harry Ammon, in "The Monroe Doctrine: Domestic Politics or National Decision," *Diplomatic History* 5 (Winter 1981): 53–70.

The simultaneous struggle with Russia over territorial claims in the Pacific Northwest is covered in the book by Saul cited above, as well as in Howard I. Kushner, *Conflict on the Northwest Coast: American-Russian Rivalry in the Pacific Northwest, 1790–1867* (Westport, Conn., 1975). The links between these negotiations and the Anglo-American discussions that led to the Monroe Doctrine are highlighted in: Howard I. Kushner, "The Russian-American Diplomatic Contest for the Pacific Basin and the Monroe Doctrine," *Journal of the West* 15 (April 1976): 65–80; and Edward P. Crapol, "John Quincy Adams and the Monroe Doctrine: Some New Evidence," *Pacific Historical Review* 48 (August 1979): 413–18.

Adams's troubled presidency forms the subject of Mary W. M. Hargreaves's *The Presidency of John Quincy Adams* (Lawrence, Kans., 1985), which covers all aspects, but highlights foreign affairs. The two volumes of Bemis's biography remain valuable for this topic, as well. Adams's tightly contested election is treated in Everett S. Brown, "The Presidential Election of 1824–1825," *Political Science Quarterly* 40 (September 1925): 384–403; and Paul C. Nagel, "The Election of 1824: A Reconsideration Based on Newspaper Opinion," *Journal of Southern History* 26 (August 1960): 315–29. The best account of Adams's "domestic" program, as laid out in his first annual address, is John Lauritz Larson, "Liberty by Design: Freedom, Planning, and John Quincy Adams's American System," in *The State and Economic Knowledge: The American and British Experiences*, ed. Mary O. Furner and Barry Supple (Cambridge, U.K., 1990), 73–102. One thing that Larson shows convincingly is that Adams's commitment to improvement was, at least initially, well received by the public—until his political opponents mobilized against it.

The same thing might be said about Adams's decision to attend the Panama Congress, as shown by Frances L. Reinhold, "New Research on the First Pan-American Congress Held at Panama in 1826," *Hispanic American Historical Review* 18 (August 1938): 342–63; Ralph Sanders, "Congressional Reaction in the United States to the Panama Congress of 1826," *The Americas* 11 (October 1954): 141–54; and Andrew R. L. Cayton, "The Debate over the Panama Congress and the Origins of the Second Party System," *The Historian* 47 (February 1985): 219–38. The emergence of the Democratic party in opposition to the Adams administration is described in numerous works; see, in particular, Richard P. McCormick, *The Second American Party System: Party Formation in the Jackson Era* (Chapel Hill, N.C., 1973). The crucial role of Martin Van Buren is recounted in

Robert V. Remini, *Martin Van Buren and the Making of the Democratic Party* (New York, 1959); and Donald B. Cole, *Martin Van Buren and the American Political System* (Princeton, N.J., 1984).

Adams's "second career" following his presidency is fully described in Bemis's second volume, but is also the particular subject of Leonard L. Richards, *The Life and Times of Congressman John Quincy Adams* (New York, 1986). Adams's efforts to serve as the family historian were not published in his own lifetime, but did appear subsequently. The published and unpublished letters and manuscripts produced by his dispute with the Federalists over the extent of New England separatism through the Hartford Convention were assembled, edited, and published by his grandson, Henry Adams, as *Documents Relating to New-England Federalism, 1800–1815* (Boston, 1877). His aborted biography of his father made up the first two chapters of Charles Francis Adams's *The Life of John Adams, Begun by John Quincy Adams, Completed by Charles Francis Adams*, 2 vols. (Philadelphia, 1871). And his abandoned history of political parties finally appeared in 1941 as *Parties in the United States* (New York, 1941).

The general political and social context in which Adams returned to political office in 1832 differed greatly from that in which he originally entered public life in 1794. Valuable general overviews of the Jacksonian Era include: Harry L. Watson, *Liberty and Power: The Politics of Jacksonian America* (New York, 1990); Charles G. Sellers, *The Market Revolution: Jacksonian America, 1815–1846* (New York, 1991); and Daniel Feller, *The Jacksonian Promise: America, 1815–1840* (Baltimore, Md., 1995). The changes in Adams's local context during these decades are thoughtfully treated in Ronald P. Formisano's *The Transformation of Political Culture: Massachusetts Parties, 1790s–1840s* (New York, 1983). Daniel Walker Howe examines the emerging Whig party, and Adams's somewhat awkward position in it, in *The Political Culture of the American Whigs* (Chicago, 1979). The Whigs', and Adams's, arch-foe during this period is the subject of two volumes by Robert V. Remini, *Andrew Jackson and the Course of American Freedom, 1822–1832* (New York, 1981) and *Andrew Jackson and the Course of American Democracy, 1833–1845* (New York, 1984).

Adams's congressional service spanned five presidential administrations, each of which is the subject of a recent study that covers domestic and foreign affairs. See Donald B. Cole, *The Presidency of Andrew Jackson* (Lawrence, Kans., 1993); Major L. Wilson, *The Presidency of Martin Van Buren* (Lawrence, Kans., 1984); Norma

Lois Peterson, *The Presidencies of William Henry Harrison and John Tyler* (Lawrence, Kans., 1989); and Paul H. Bergeron, *The Presidency of James K. Polk* (Lawrence, Kans., 1987). Adams returned to politics amidst the union-threatening nullification crisis, which is carefully analyzed in Richard E. Ellis, *The Union at Risk: Jacksonian Democracy, States' Rights and the Nullification Crisis* (New York, 1987). Key works on the foreign affairs of this period include: David M. Pletcher, *The Diplomacy of Annexation: Texas, Oregon, and the Mexican War* (Columbia, Mo., 1973); John M. Belohlavek, *"Let the Eagle Soar!": The Foreign Policy of Andrew Jackson* (Lincoln, Neb., 1985); and Thomas R. Hietala, *Manifest Design: Anxious Aggrandizement in Late Jacksonian America* (Ithaca, N.Y., 1985).

During the last decade or so of his life, Adams battled against the "slave power" on a number of issues, domestic and foreign. His leading role in the fight against the "gag rule" is discussed in Lynn Hudson Parsons, "Censuring Old Man Eloquent," *Capitol Studies* 3 (Fall 1973): 89–106; David C. Frederick, "John Quincy Adams, Slavery, and the Disappearance of the Right of Petition," *Law and History Review* 9 (Spring 1991): 113–55; and, especially, William Lee Miller, *Arguing About Slavery: John Quincy Adams and the Great Battle in the United States Congress* (New York, 1996). Howard Jones chronicles Adams's participation in the legal struggle to free the Africans of the *Amistad* in *Mutiny on the "Amistad": The Saga of a Slave Revolt and Its Impact on American Abolition* (New York, 1987). Adams's battle against the Jackson, Van Buren, Tyler, and Polk administrations over territorial expansion is well handled by Bemis, but is also set into a broader context by Kinley Brauer, *Cotton versus Conscience: Massachusetts Whig Politics and Southwestern Expansion* (Lexington, Ky., 1967), and Michael A. Morrison, *Slavery and the American West: The Eclipse of Manifest Destiny and the Coming of the Civil War* (Chapel Hill, N.C., 1997). For a provocative effort to reconceive and rehabilitate Tyler's foreign policy, see Edward P. Crapol, "John Tyler and the Pursuit of National Destiny," *Journal of the Early Republic* 17 (Fall 1997): 467–91. Even though he fought against slavery and the "slave power" on many fronts, Adams's ideas about race lagged behind those of many abolitionists, as William Jerry MacLean shows in "Othello Scorned: The Racial Thought of John Quincy Adams," *Journal of the Early Republic* 4 (Summer 1984): 143–60.

Adams's death produced a nationwide response, rivaled by that of few nineteenth-century Americans. Parsons's bibliography cited above provides entries for thirty-two eulogies, orations, and other remembrances. He has also published a full account of the reaction to Adams's death: "The 'Splendid Pageant': Observations on the Death of John Quincy Adams," *New England Quarterly* 53 (December 1980): 464–82.

Index

Abolitionism, 82, 126–28, 131
Adams, Abigail, 2–4
Adams, Charles Francis, 122, 136
Adams, George Washington, 12, 121–22
Adams, John, 1–5, 7, 12, 14, 120–22
Adams, John (son), 122
Adams, John Quincy: "Columbus" essays, 7, 10; commencement address, 5–6; on Constitution, 5–8, 16, 34, 37–38, 49, 134, 137; continentalism, 35, 51, 60, 67, 142, 144; death, 136–37; depression, 99, 108, 112–13; *Duplicate Letters*, 75; early influences on, 1–5, 17; education, 2–5; on expansion, 44, 47, 51–52, 60, 67, 72, 103, 142, 144; as Federalist, 6, 13–17, 23–24; first annual message, 101, 103, 107, 111, 143; Fourth of July oration (1821), 86–87; Fourth of July oration (1831), 124; inaugural address, 99–101, 103, 143; and Jay's Treaty, 12; as lawyer, 5, 7, 26; and lessons of War of 1812, 21–22, 30, 33, 38–39, 100; on Louisiana Purchase, 1, 13–16; "Marcellus" essays, 10–11; marriage, 11–12; as minister to Great Britain, 21, 30–31; as minister to the Netherlands, 7–8, 10, 12; as minister to Prussia, 1, 8, 12; as minister to Russia, 21–22, 26; on neutrality, 6–7, 10–11, 38–39, 54, 105–7; on noninterventionism, 86, 91; on parties, 10, 13, 35, 73, 102–3, 108; on peace, 30–34, 39, 43–45, 47–48, 60, 67, 72, 141–42;

personality, 12, 16–17, 29, 64, 74; on policymaking, 10–11, 16–17, 21–22, 37–39, 47–52, 55–56, 64, 67, 72, 137, 142–43; on post-Napoleonic Europe, 30–34, 39; as president, 99–116, 124, 129, 141–44; as representative, 119–38; as Republican, 22–24, 73; on republican government, 1, 6, 9–11, 13, 16–17, 21, 29–30, 36–38, 43–44, 48, 80, 144; retirement, 119–22; as secretary of state, 43–68, 71–95, 141–45; as senator, 14–16, 22–26; on "slave power," 120, 123, 126–27, 129–32, 137–38, 144–45; on slavery, 81, 120, 126–29, 144; and Treaty of Ghent, 21–22, 28–29; on union, 1, 6–10, 13, 16–17, 21–22, 24, 30–31, 35–37, 39, 43–44, 51, 61, 66–67, 72, 101–3, 113–16, 120, 123–24, 126–28, 131–33, 137–38, 141–45; Young Men's Whig Club address, 133
Adams, Louisa Catherine, 11–12, 122–23, 137–38
Adams-Onís Treaty. *See* Transcontinental Treaty
Alexander I of Russia, 26
Ambrister, Robert, 55, 57
Amelia Island, 54
American System, 101–2, 108
Amistad case, 126, 131
Anderson, Richard C., 88–89, 112
Anti-Masons, 124–25
Arbuthnot, Alexander, 55, 57
Austria, 86, 89

Bagot, Charles, 52–53
Bayard, James A., 28

Bolívar, Simón, 106
Brazil, 105, 109–10
Breckinridge, John, 15
Buenos Aires, 54, 56, 87–88, 90, 105

Calhoun, John C., 34, 108, 111–12, 123, 133; as secretary of war, 46, 50, 54, 56, 63, 71, 75–76, 79, 90
California, 90, 135
Canada, 25, 27–29, 33, 45, 53, 59, 78, 134
Canning, Stratford, 65–66, 80–81
Castlereagh, Viscount, 31, 47
Central American federation, 105, 109
Chesapeake affair, 21–23
Chile, 87, 90–91
Clay, Henry, 31, 34, 38, 71, 73–76, 125–26, 133, 137; as secretary of state, 99–103, 105–7, 109–11, 113–15, 119, 129; and Spanish American affairs, 54–57, 64–66, 86–87, 92; and Treaty of Ghent, 28
Colombia, 87–88, 91, 93, 106
Columbia River, 65, 94
Commerce, 31, 45, 47, 51–53, 58–59, 71, 77–80, 84, 94, 104–6, 109–10, 112, 142–43; and European wars, 21–26; and Spanish America, 47, 88–89, 94, 105–6, 109–10, 143
Constitution, 5–8, 16
Convention of 1815, 31, 45, 59, 78–79, 145
Convention of 1818, 44, 52, 58–61, 65, 79, 93, 104, 145
"Corrupt bargain," 101, 110
Crawford, William H., 50, 64, 71, 73, 75–76, 79, 82–83, 101, 103, 111
Creek Indians, 46, 55
Crowninshield, Benjamin, 50
Cuba, 103–4, 106, 113–14, 131–32

Democrats, 100, 107–8, 110–12, 116, 121, 123–26, 131, 133–34, 143
de Tuyll van Serooskerken, Hendrik, 89, 91

Diplomatic recognition. *See* Recognition
Disunionism, 15, 24–30, 34, 121, 128

Election of 1800, 10, 13
Election of 1824, 71–77, 87, 95, 99, 101–2, 110, 145. *See also* "Corrupt bargain"
Election of 1828, 99, 112, 115, 119
Election of 1844, 133–34
Embargo, 21–26

Federalists, 6–8, 13–17, 23, 25–29, 73, 102, 121
Filibustering, 38, 47–49, 65–66
Fisheries, 47, 51, 53, 59
Florida: East, 14, 46–48, 53–60, 63–64, 67; West, 14, 46
Floyd, John, 65
Founders, 1, 5–9, 21, 66–67, 85, 87, 94, 100, 108, 113–16
France, 6–8, 21, 23, 26, 48, 52, 64, 66, 86, 89–93, 95, 104, 106, 114, 125, 142–43; commercial convention, 77–79, 84, 95, 143, 145; and Louisiana Purchase, 14, 16
Freemasonry. *See* Anti-Masons

"Gag rule," 126, 128–29, 131,138
Gallatin, Albert, 25, 28–29, 31, 58–59, 79
Great Britain, 7–8, 21–27, 31, 33, 45–47, 52–53, 58, 60, 63, 67, 77–80, 83–84, 93–95, 104–6, 114, 132, 134–35, 137, 141–43; colonial markets, 31, 45, 47, 58, 77–80, 83–84, 104–6, 110, 112, 143; and Monroe Doctrine, 90–95; and War of 1812, 22, 27–29, 38. *See also* Convention of 1815; Convention of 1818; Oregon; Slave trade convention

Hamilton, Alexander, 1, 6, 8
Harrison, William Henry, 132
Hartford Convention, 28
Holy Alliance, 86, 89–94
Home market, 35–36. *See also* American System
Hyde de Neuville, Guillaume, 52–53, 56, 58, 64, 66, 79

Impressment, 23–24, 26–27, 29, 31, 33, 45, 58–59, 81–83
Indians, 29, 33, 38, 45–47, 123, 129–30, 144

Jackson, Andrew, 54–58, 63, 71, 74, 76, 101, 103, 107–8, 111; as president, 99, 116, 119, 123–26, 128–31, 135, 137, 143–44
Jay's Treaty, 12
Jefferson, Thomas, 1, 6, 12–13, 15–16, 23–24

King, Rufus, 83, 105–6, 110

Lafayette, Marquis de, 92
Louisiana Purchase, 13–16, 46

Madison, James, 1, 6, 8–9; as president, 26–27, 31–32, 34, 38, 86, 141–42; as secretary of state, 15–16
Manifest Destiny, 134
Mexican War, 120, 132, 135–36, 138
Mexico, 87, 90, 93, 105–6, 109–10, 113–14, 129–30, 132–36
Mississippi River, 14–16, 103
Missouri Crisis, 44, 61–63, 67, 71, 87, 126
Monroe, James, 23; as president, 43–47, 50, 52, 54, 56–57, 59, 63–65, 71, 73, 76, 79–80, 84–95, 132, 141–42; as secretary of state, 31–32, 34, 38
Monroe Doctrine, 85, 89–95, 105, 114, 143, 145
Most-favored-nation status, 78, 89, 109

National Republicans, 124–25
Native Americans. *See* Indians
Neutrality legislation, 55
Neutral rights: and Europe, 10–12, 23–24, 26–27, 29, 31, 33, 45, 58–59, 77, 83–84, 104; and Spanish America, 88–89, 104, 107
New England, 7, 14, 24–25, 28–29
New Mexico, 136
Non-Intercourse Act, 25–26
Nullification, 121, 123–24, 144

Onís, Luis de, 52–53, 55–60, 63
Oregon, 45, 47, 53, 59–60, 65–67, 93–94, 104, 120, 132, 134–35, 137–38, 142

Panama Congress, 106–7, 109, 112, 114–15, 143
Panic of 1819, 44, 61–63, 67, 87
Peru, 87, 90
Pickering, Timothy, 12
Pinkney, William, 23
Poinsett, Joel R., 105, 109–10
Polk, James K., 132–37
Portugal, 48–49, 109
Privateering, 11–12, 38, 47–49, 54, 65–66, 84
Puerto Rico, 104, 106

Quasi–War, 11

Raguet, Condy, 110
Reciprocity, 78–79, 84, 89, 104–6, 109, 143
Recognition, 54–57, 65–66, 86–88, 90, 94, 104–5, 143, 145
Republicans, 6–8, 13, 15, 23, 27, 34–37, 73, 102, 110
Rodney, Caesar A., 88–89
Rush, Richard, 58–59, 82–83, 89, 91–92, 132
Rush-Bagot Agreement, 31, 46, 145
Russell, Jonathan, 28, 74–75
Russia, 26, 64–66, 77, 86, 89–91, 93–94, 106, 114, 142, 145; northwest boundary convention with, 93–94, 142, 145

Seminole Indians, 46–47, 54–55
Sergeant, John, 112
Seward, William Henry, 136
Slave trade convention, 71, 77, 80–84, 143, 145
South, 7, 14, 62–63, 82–83, 126–33, 136–38, 144
Southard, Samuel L., 103
Spain, 14, 33, 60, 66, 86, 89, 131, 142; and Spanish American revolutions, 33, 38, 47–48, 53–58, 65–66, 86–90, 104–6, 109–10, 113–14; territorial negotiations, 45–47, 52–60, 63–67, 71, 93,

Spain (*continued*)
142. *See also* Transcontinental
Treaty
Spanish America: post-indepen-
dence, 85, 87–95, 100, 104–7,
109–10, 114–15, 143; revolutions
in, 33, 38, 45, 47–48, 53–54, 56,
58, 65, 71, 85–87, 143. *See also*
Recognition
Sumner, Charles, 136
Sweden, 105, 109

Tariffs, 36–37, 101, 108, 113, 123,
125, 135, 144; Tariff of 1828, 108,
113
Taylor, Zachary, 135
Texas, 46–48, 53, 65, 103–5, 109–
10, 113–14; annexation of, 120,
126, 129–35, 137–38; and

Transcontinental Treaty, 55, 57,
60, 63, 65, 67, 129
Transcontinental Treaty, 44, 52,
55, 58–61, 63–67, 71, 85–86, 93,
129, 145
Treaty of Ghent, 29, 31, 33, 38, 45,
53, 59, 74, 145
Tyler, John, 132–35, 137

Van Buren, Martin, 108, 111, 126,
129–31, 135, 137

War of 1812, 21–22, 26–29, 46–47
Washington, George, 1, 7, 10
Webster, Daniel, 125–26
West, 7, 14–15
Whigs, 121, 124–25, 133, 143
Wilmot Proviso, 136
Wirt, William, 50, 103

ISBN 0-8420-2622-3

9 780842 026222

90000 >